GUIDE TO BETTER GARDENING

LANDSCAPE GARDENING

Editor: Margaret Verner
Dust Jacket designed by Roswita Busskamp
Copyright © 1981 by 'Round the World Books Inc.

Landscape Gardening published by
Galahad Books Inc., New York City.

This edition published by arrangement with
'Round the World Books Inc., New York, N.Y.

Library of Congress Catalog Card Number: 79-56675

ISBN: 0-88365-436-9

Printed in the United States of America

PICTURE ACKNOWLEDGEMENTS:

A.B. Morse: 96 — Bristol Nurseries Inc.: 7, 65 — E.A. Fisher, Downsview, Ontario: 87 — Emerson Industries, Hempstead, N.Y.: 74, 75, 76 — George J. Ball Inc.: 31L, 33L — Imperial Landscaping, Erindale, Ontario: 8, 9, 11, 12, 15, 16, 19, 31R, 32, 37TR, 37BR, 38T, 51, 59, 62, 85, 86, 88, 89 — Jackson & Perkins Co.: 54R — Keith Seed Co.: 60 — Kelly Bros.: 26, 27, 28, 29T — Lord and Burnham: 69, 70, 71, 72T, 72B, 73T, 73B, 77T, 77BL, 77BR, 78T, 78BR, 78BL, 79T, 79B — McConnell Nurseries: 25, 38BL — Nova Scotia Department of Travel: 30 — Ontario Agricultural College: 37TL, 37BL, 68L — Ontario Horitcultural Association: 6, 35, 68C — Patmore Nurseries: 48R — Sheridan Nurseries: 38BR, 48TL, 48BL, 68R — Stokes Seed Co.: 33R, 36, 50, 54L — Union Pacific Railroad: 10, 29, 57 — Vaughan's Seed Co.: 18, 20, 21, 24 — W. Atlee Burpee Seed Co., Philadelphia, Pa.: 81, 82 — W.B. Cross, Galt, Ontario: 80 — W. Crawford, Galt, Ontario: 83, 90L, 90TR, 90BR, 91T, 91B, 92T, 92B, 93TL, 93TR, 93B, 94T, 94B, 95.

Table of Contents

HOME LANDSCAPING

HOME LANDSCAPING

Landscaping is laying out a property according to a definite plan

All about landscaping

Few home owners appreciate the difference between simple planting and landscaping. They do not realize the latter is really a step ahead — the laying out of a property according to a definite plan.

As a result, not many homes are actually landscaped. Instead, the owner sets out trees, shrubs and other plants in a haphazard way wherever he can find room to place them. The result of this **disorderly** handling is a sort of vegetable chop suey in which no single specimen has a chance to contribute its full order and beauty to the whole picture.

When asked why they do not landscape according to plan, many owners reply, "But it costs too much". They are thinking, of course, of the professional landscape architect who works on a fee over and above the charge made by a landscape nurseryman

for planting the stock specified. What they fail to realize is that even professional landscape treatment is not an expense — it is an investment. True, a home owner may not be able to make that investment, but he should not forego landscaping for that reason.

Home owners who do not hesitate to spend thousands of dollars for automatic laundry equipment, air conditioning units, kitchen devices and other conveniences overlook the fact that the moment any of these **appliances is installed, it will immediately depreciate. Even driving a new automobile around the block will drop its value considerably.**

Consider how landscaping differs from these luxury items. A well-designed planting can immediately add as much as $5,000 to the value of an average home. Each year, instead of deteriorating, shrubs and trees

increase in value as they grow to maturity. Real estate men often place a price of as much as $500 to $1,000 on a single tree. Perhaps the most skeptical men in the world — income tax authorities — recognize this same value and allow substantial deductions when landscape material is destroyed by fire or storm.

Professional services seldom available—A landscape architect can seldom be persuaded to design a property of modest size. His fee is based on a percentage of cost, so that if the price of a finished job is much less than $10,000 he can not afford to touch it. Even at this figure he would much rather design for schools, libraries, factories and other non-home jobs, since the work is much simpler and he has fewer service calls after the job is finished.

Landscape nurserymen — Because of fees charged by trained landscape architects, most home plantings in the $2,000 to $5,000 range are designed and planted by landscape nurserymen. These are men who both make plans and sell nursery stock. Most of them employ men trained as landscape architects who draw up simple designs for less elaborate plantings.

In theory, the architect is supposed to have a more professional detachment from the plant material used, but in practice the landscape nurseryman grows material especially fitted to his needs and often does a more imaginative job than his professional competitor.

He works in a number of ways. Sometimes, but not often nowadays, he makes a rough drawing of a property without charge in anticipation of selling the job. More often, he may charge a fee for his preliminary work, which may or may not be refunded if he is awarded the job.

If an extensive house planting costing a thousand dollars or more is contemplated it will pay to consult a landscape nurseryman. Always insist upon seeing several jobs he has planted in your community to see if his work meets your approval.

Do-it-yourself landscaping — Many home owners with limited funds find it necessary to do their own planning and planting. If they will pay attention to details of good design and workmanship, even a beginner can turn out a presentable landscape plan and execute it.

On buying books on the subject of landscaping, however, they are often confronted by strange, unfamiliar terms such as focal points, major and minor axis lines, orientation, etc. These books were not written for the home owner but deal with the design of extensive estates, parks, cemeteries and other large public areas. The problem of the home owner is entirely different; he is concerned with laying out a small space in orderly fashion and in doing so, providing privacy, useable space and beauty.

While a small city lot or even a larger suburban property may need a central axis along which to center the plan, there is seldom room for any more elaborate development. Few properties offer much in the way of a view other than that of a neighbour's picture window or his back door. Naturally, where some pleasant or dramatic scene can be framed by planting on a property, thus making it a part of the landscape picture, common sense would dictate that this be done. In general, however, it is safe to say that a small property owner should limit his efforts to the area within the property line.

First principles — Owners of houses already built can do nothing about location, orientation, etc., of the building. Even those who are in the house planning stage have most of these questions answered for them by municipal ordinances. To waste time describing the advantages of one exposure over another would be of little help to 99 out of 100 home owners planning their homes.

Although there might be real advantages in setting a house back from the street, to do so would reduce the potential sales value if it must be sold later. Custom compels home owners to observe the set building line. Nor does it pay to consider an unorthodox placement of rooms; no matter how many arguments may be given for placing the living room to the rear, facing the garden and the kitchen on the street side, that too, renders a house less saleable.

About the only major item over which a prospective builder has some control is the location of the driveway. Today, most landscape designs automatically call for this feature since the automobile is a fixed part of North American life. Unfortunately, this creates an ugly area of low interest, occupying conspicuous space and a trap for heat and dust.

If at all possible, locate the drive on the north side of a house. If on the south, heat reflected from the pavement can often increase temperatures inside by several degrees or cause air conditioning units to work harder.

If in addition to the drive, a walk to the front door must be incorporated in the design, not much is left of the front lawn on a 50 to 60 foot city lot. A good solution for this problem is to combine the walk and drive. The latter can also serve as a service walk to the kitchen door and to the rear of the property.

Do give consideration to entering the back lawn and garden from the street. Often a rotary tiller or power mower must be brought from front to rear and if not enough space is allowed for passageway, skinned knuckles will call attention to the mistake in planning. To allow for most equipment, leave 42 inches between the house and garage if the path goes between them.

Whenever possible, provide space for off-street parking of one or two cars for visitors and service men.

On the south side of a house, allow six feet of space between drive and house so there will be room for adequate planting. On the north side, however, this may not be desirable with a two story house, although with a one story house there should be enough light for a good planting. In the case of the former, a narrow strip which will give enough root room for vines to go against

Always insist on seeing several jobs of a landscape nurseryman before you sign a contract

the wall is one solution.

Before you build — Sometimes it is inconvenient to do any landscape planning until after the house is completed. However, the following points must be considered before excavating for the house:-

1. Will the proposed house location take advantage of existing trees and have an attractive view.
2. If you are fortunate enough to have trees growing on your lot, protect them from heavy equipment damage by building a wooden guard around them.
3. Separate the top-soil from the sub-soil. Leave a 20 foot working area around the house. Endeavour to be present when the excavating is being done and instruct the operator of the bulldozer or steam shovel to pile the top-soil and sub-soil in separate piles to the sides or the back of the property.
4. Stake out the driveway location. While the bulldozer is on the property excavating your basement, have the top-soil removed from the proposed driveway. Heavy equipment running over the driveway area will help to firm and consolidate the base.

Placing of the house on the lot—It is most important to remember that water runs downhill, so beware of low lying areas. If possible inspect the lot during wet weather, especially during Spring break-up. The higher a house is set on the lot, the less excavation will be needed, but a natural grade is better than a man-made one. You should ask yourself, "Can the house location be altered to avoid expensive grading jobs?"

In choosing the location for the house, be sure to allow enough space for the driveway, garage or breeze-way and for a flower border or shrub planting between the house and the drive.

The position of the house on the lot should allow for sufficient level space for the septic tank and field bed if you live in an area where there are no sewers. You should also allow enough space for a hedge, fence or shrubs border between the driveway and the edge of the property.

If your lot is located on a heavily travelled road you should think seriously about a turncourt, so that you will not have to back out into traffic.

If at all possible, locate the driveway on the north side of the house

Orientation of the house — We not only have to worry about the correct location of the house on the property, but should also think very seriously about the plan of the house itself.

1. Consider sunlight in the kitchen and living-room.
2. Is the morning sun going to shine into your bedroom.
3. Does the bathroom give your neighbour an excellent view.
4. Consider the views when looking through the windows — for instance, are you looking at a neighbour's garage, or some other unsightly scene. If you are spending the money on a picture window, you should have something to see, or else have the possibilities for creating a picture.
5. Make use of existing trees, allowing shade during the Summer and sunlight in the Winter.

Fill—When planning the landscaping of a new property, try to make "cut equal fill". That is, try to keep the amount of filling needed down to the volume of the soil that will be dug out of the foundation hole or scraped off high spots and driveways. This reduces the cost of fill, since no clay or dirt has to be removed from the property and

also avoids the expense of bringing these in.

Sometimes fill cannot be avoided. Lots along ravines, creeks or in other places where levels change rapidly may be unusable unless large volumes of soil, clay or rock can be had at low cost. Perhaps the most neglected low-cost material of all are steam cinders. These are produced when coal is burned at high temperatures in power plants. They are a drug on the market and can usually be had for the cost of hauling. For deep fill, they can be used "as is" but if they can be purchased a year or two ahead of actual operations, should be stock piled outside to weather. This removes certain sulfur impurities and other chemicals that might injure plant roots if they come in contact (not a problem with deep fill).

When weathered, steam cinders can be screened through a $\frac{1}{4}$ inch mesh (16 holes to the square inch) and the fine material used as part of the top soil in the lawn and garden. This makes a better soil additive than most other materials.

Clay is difficult to use unless drainage is good. If the property has little slope, drainage tile may be needed if only clay can be had for fill. A better material is what is known as road gravel—the rough unwashed upper layers taken off a gravel pit. This contains both fine and rough, as well as just

Consider the views created when looking through the windows

create landscape pictures.

The owner is fortunate who can start even before the first spadeful of earth is turned for the foundation. If he owns a lot which will not be used for building for a year or two, this is a golden opportunity to build up the black soil on the surface of the property, to destroy weeds and perhaps to make preliminary fill on areas which need to be raised in level.

Drainage — Few properties are so well situated that drainage can be ignored. Inside city limits, storm sewers may carry away excess water, but if the slope of a lawn leads water towards the foundation instead of away from it, a damp or flooded basement can still occur. Raised flower beds may solve a problem of growing plants in low spots, but if they are built across the natural drainage of the area, wet spots can develop.

The first step in considering drainage is to imagine what will happen to a barrel filled with water after it has been upset in the middle of a property. Where will it flow? What is the natural outlet for such excess water? Do not try to judge this while standing erect; lie down on the ground and sight away from the house on all four sides.

enough clay to keep water from rushing through it rapidly, yet is coarse enough to provide perfect drainage. Since this material is not washed and graded it is usually quite low in cost.

Black dirt is the most variable of all materials used for fill or topdressing. It seldom comes from a rich garden area. More likely it is taken from a swamp of little value for farming or from worn out fields. Or it may be scraped from land being developed by a speculative builder. About the only sure thing about it is that it contains weed seeds and roots.

Sometimes the owner is compelled to buy black soil, but should avoid doing so whenever possible. If building a new home, he should have a provision written into the excavation contract that no top soil can be removed from the property without written permission. This will prevent the theft from him of an asset that has taken ages to build up. Top soil should be piled away from clay or gravel from the cellar hole. If weeds cover it, use a chemical to kill these before they set seed.

That part of the black soil pile used for the upper four inches of lawn should be treated with a weed-killing chemical when air temperatures are above 70 degrees. Your

For better drainage, connect downspout to dry well

local garden center will recommend a soil fumigant approved for use in your locality.

As much as possible, avoid the use of bull-dozers in grading. For deep fill, they save hours of labor and dollars in cost, but at the expense of compacting soil and destroying the natural drainage. Try to do the final levelling with a wheel barrow or similar light equipment.

Construction — Basis of good landscaping — The difference between haphazard planting and true landscaping lies largely in the use of special construction to

Be sure that if a cloudburst does occur, as is possible in the eastern half of the United States and Canada, the water it releases will have some place to go. If it does not, try to provide that runoff.

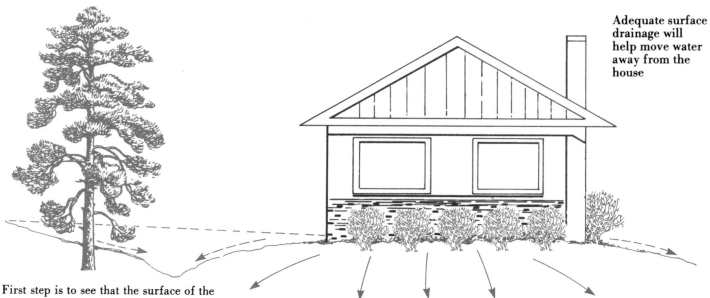

Adequate surface drainage will help move water away from the house

First step is to see that the surface of the property slopes away from the foundation at a rate of one-eighth to one-fourth of an inch to each foot. This means that if the house stands fifty feet from the street, it should be at least six inches above the curb line at the foundation, but if possible, not more than a foot higher. A sharper slope means possible washing and erosion.

If proper drainage is not possible by sloping the surface, underground drains may have to be laid, using clay tile or perforated fiber pile to lead excess water away from the property to a lower point. Sometimes, city ordinances will allow drain tile to be attached to storm sewers. If not, an outlet must be provided in some way to take off excess water.

If no other outlet is possible, tiles can be drained into a dry well, which is nothing more than a big hole, lower than the tile outlet and filled with coarse stone or gravel. This blots up the excess water until it can drain away or evaporate from the surface. One way to get rid of water rapidly from a dry well is to plant a weeping willow nearby. It will evaporate at least a barrel of water a day.

Making the correct grade — In any new home the foundation and the curb or sidewalk level are the fixed grade points. In doing the grading, we want to arrange the soil between these fixed points into gradual pleasant slopes. These should lead any excess water away from the house and off the property.

The lawn should, if possible, slope gradually away from the house to adjacent property, sidewalk or road. Any height that needs losing should be lost at the road or

sidewalk edge rather than close to the house. In all too many cases, the earth is mounded up around the house in the form of terraces which merely serve to push the house up into the air instead of blending it easily into the landscape.

You will recall that early in the book we said that the top-soil should be pushed off to the side of the property ready for use later on. Before using this soil you must first of all level out and grade the sub-soil. Then spread the top-soil evenly over the sub-soil.

Many new home owners want to know if it is necessary to haul in top-soil if it is not already on the property. If you do not have too many money problems, there is no doubt that this would be a good plan. However, for the young couple who have just bought a new house, it may prove a bit too costly. It will take a little more trouble, but you can still build a good lawn using the soil already on the property, unless it is stony, gravelly or the heaviest kind of poor subsoil. In buying top soil the top six inches from a farm pasture or crop land is the only kind to use.

As mentioned earlier in the book, the upper four inches of the soil used for lawn —whether it be the earth already there, or top soil hauled in—should be treated with a weed-killing chemical when air temperatures are above 70 degrees. Materials used for this purpose include vapan, dowfume or methyl bromide and calcium cyanamide. Not all garden centers or seed stores will carry these chemicals, but they will certainly be only too pleased to order them for you.

Final grading — With all underfill and drainage in place, topsoil can be dumped over the area ready for final grading. When this has been spaded and raked fairly level, one section of a wooden extension ladder can be used as a drag or land plane to bring it to a uniform surface. A rope is tied to both top and bottom rung and the ladder section dragged by this rope across the surface in all directions.

As the side rail is pulled along, it will

The lawn should slope away from the house gradually

pick up earth from high spots and deposit it in low spots. Several passes with the improvised drag will leave a near-level surface, and the job should be ready for planting.

Spot trees — The time to make provisions for new trees is when grading is being done. Their roots may travel for forty to fifty feet when mature, but if a fill of rich black dirt six to eight feet deep and about as wide as can be provided for their early years of growth, the extra work needed to provide this will be well repaid. A well-planted tree will make double the early growth of one which must forage for a living through poor soil.

Existing trees offer a real problem if any amount of fill will be needed. Even as little as six inches of extra soil over the roots of a maple, for example, can smother it and cause its death. Tap rooted trees such as black walnut are better able to survive under fill, yet should not be subjected to this abuse if it can be avoided.

Where fill is essential, the area under the tree, out to the drip from the ends of the branches, should be covered with coarse, airy fill, such as crushed granite, hard gravel, the coarse screenings from steam cinders or similar material, to a depth of about six inches. Any surface fill can then go over this, even if three or four feet deep.

Around the trunk of the tree, build a retaining wall about 18 inches to 24 inches away from the trunk on all sides, to the depth of the fill. If necessary to avoid a pitfall for children, this can be filled with coarse gravel but is better left unfilled.

Existing trees—Few owners are so fortunate as to own lots on which existing trees must be considered. All too often, the best tree grows on the exact spot which city regulations dictate the house must stand. If it is not too large, and if it is of a species which should be planted, consider having a landscaper move it for you. Trees are seldom situated exactly right on a property, but unless they are so badly placed that they cannot be fitted into the design, try to figure what can be done to make them conform to the general scheme. For example, if a fine oak is about ten feet too far to one side, often planting a clump of smaller trees, such as hawthorns or flowering crabs to the opposite side will have the effect of pulling the mass of the entire group into place.

Be sure to read what is said elsewhere in

Try to fit the location of the house so that existing trees are not disturbed

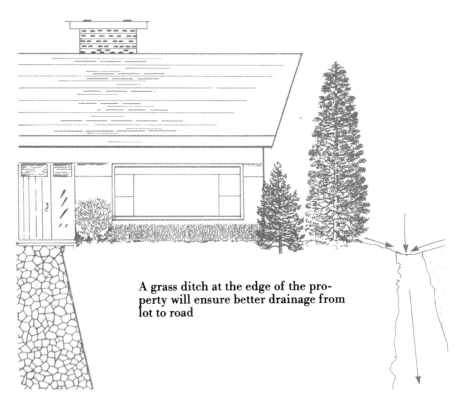

A grass ditch at the edge of the property will ensure better drainage from lot to road

this book about fill over trees, in case a change in level is made.

Making out the plan—It is a good idea to make this a family project. Discuss with your family what they expect from the property and list these desired items on a sheet of paper; e.g.

Flower border

Children's play area

The foundation and the sidewalk level are the fixed grade points

Vegetable garden   Barbecue etc.
Clothes line

With the features in mind which are to be incorporated in the finished landscape scheme, the next step is to lay out these elements in an orderly, attractive manner. A real help in making the plan is graph paper —a ruled paper divided into small squares, available at most stationery stores. Use the 18″ x 24″ size or larger. Allow one square to represent a foot, or some convenient unit, and lay out the property in exact scale.

Next, draw in permanent fixtures such as the house, garage, drive and existing trees that are to be saved. Do not guess at their location—measure exactly. An investment in a good steel tape of 100 foot length will certainly pay off. In the case of big trees, be sure to indicate the diameter of the top with dotted lines, not just the small circle for the trunk.

The next step is to estimate the sizes of the features you have listed as desirable. An experienced landscape architect usually draws a rough circle about the size of the area needed for each feature, and then erases and juggles these around until he is satisfied with the arrangement of all the elements. However, an amateur will find it much easier to draw out each feature to the same scale as the plan on graph paper.

Remember, the area in front of your house should be simple and attractive. The recreational space, which is usually located behind the house, should be screened on all sides. The vegetable garden is placed further back on the property, or may extend from behind the garage.

Now is the time to consider circulation or traffic movement through your property
    —Where does the garbage pail go?
    —Where will the car be left when not in the garage?
    —How will guests reach the barbecue area from the street?
    —Where will you place the tool-house, incinerator, compost pile, etc.?

After asking a few questions of this sort, it will be probably clear that certain features must be moved around to provide better circulation, and to avoid wear and tear of the lawn.

From the list of desired items you wish to have on your property, make a start by inserting the largest items in your plan first. This would include the lawn area, vegetable garden, children's play area and boundary plantings of hedges or fences.

After the larger items have been placed, complete your plan by inserting the smaller items such as shade trees, foundation plantings, flower borders, rose arbors, etc.

Land must slope away from the home in all directions despite rolling topography

1. A real help in making the plan is graph paper—a ruled paper divided into small squares.

2. Draw in permanent fixtures such as the house, garage, drive and existing trees.

3. The completed plan should include the lawn area, vegetable garden, children's play area and boundary plantings.

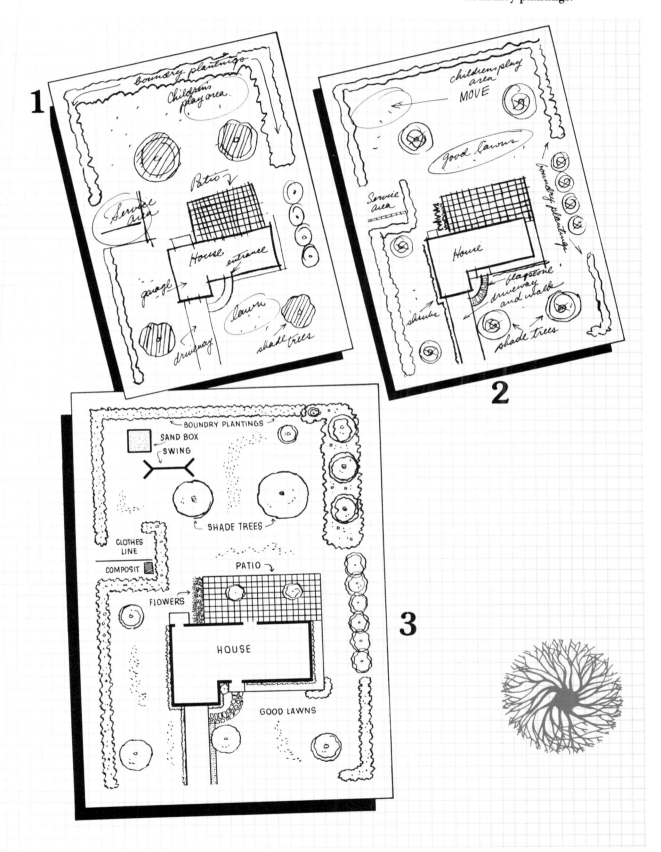

Semi~formal arrangement

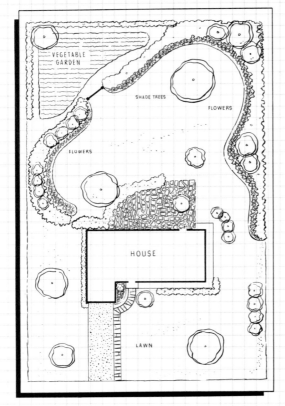

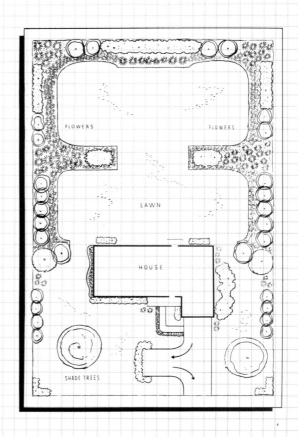

Formal garden

A patio can be a charming place to entertain outdoors

Features to include

Outdoor dining—Today, facilities for outdoor dining, cooking and entertaining are so popular that even if not wanted by the present owner, space for them should be provided in case the property is ever put up for sale.

All too often, barbecue grilles are built, used once or twice with a great flourish but then allowed to sit idle. There are two drawbacks to their regular use — rain and flying pests such as flies and mosquitoes. For this reason, serious consideration should be given to paving an area along the back or one side of the garage, over which a roof can be erected and the enclosed area screened. Such an enclosed porch can be used in rainy weather or when flying pests make life unbearable in the open. Too, with very little additional work, plastic can be tacked over the screens so the porch can be used in Spring or late in the Fall.

The fireplace or grille itself should be built on the outside edge of the paved slab rather than against the garage wall. Be sure to extend the chimney at least two feet above the highest point on the garage roof.

Play areas—Most city and suburban lots are too small to allow for such sports as tennis, crouquet, volleyball and badminton, unless the owner is willing to sacrifice most of his lawn area. Do not overlook the possibilities of using the driveway, particularly if paved with concrete or blacktop, for sports that can be played in a long, narrow area. Darts, horseshoe pitching, archery and shuffleboard are among these. Directions for laying out courts, etc., can be obtained from books on these sports.

Most boys love to shoot baskets: a backstop on top of the garage will allow the use of the driveway for this healthy exercise without interfering with other sports played there.

Laying out the plan—Curves drawn on paper may or may not look equally well when laid out on the soil, ready for planting. One of the most useful gadgets for laying out curves is an ordinary garden hose. Place this along the proposed line, curved about as planned, then stand off and look at the effect. Often shifting the line only a trifle will make a much better curve. Mistakes in layout are harder to correct once lawns, shrubs and walks are permanently placed.

One difficult thing for the amateur to do is to visualize the mass of a certain shrub. He may know it grows six feet high and has a spread of four feet, but these dimensions are hard to picture without some tangible guide. Bushel baskets or cardboard cartons of the approximate size are handy guides to the amount of space a given shrub will fill. Several baskets can be piled up to give a bigger mass.

For larger specimens, sometimes a frame of light sticks can be tacked together to show the final height of big shrubs and small trees. These dummies will prevent misplacing specimen plants so they are either hidden by other material and their value lost, or so they stand out more than they should.

Planting — The time has come to translate the paper plan into actual landscaping. Here two facts must be kept in mind — the immediate effect of woody plants and their final habit and stature. It is a temptation to overplant for early effect, with the idea of removing some of the shrubs later. This seldom works out well; the extra specimens are too much trouble to remove and stay in place permanently. Stick to the plan as originally drawn, leaving what seems to be too much room around each. If this leaves the planting too thin and bare, use annuals to fill in rather than woody plant material.

One of the most useful of all annuals for massive temporary effects is the castor bean, which can produce a twelve to fifteen foot plant in a single Summer if grown in rich soil. Planted behind a sapling tree for a year or two, it fills in the background beautifully (one important fact to remember, however, is that the beans or seeds of castor bean are poisonous if swallowed and must be kept away from children). Taller marigolds, tithonia, cleome and other tall growing annuals can be used to give a more finished effect to the shrubbery border.

Actual planting — It is important to remember that every tree and shrub is being set where it will remain for years to come. Once it is growing, it cannot be easily dug up and given a change of soil. Preparation of the planting hole is perhaps the most important single step in landscaping: how well it is done determines what will happen to every specimen used.

The old saying, "Better a 50c shrub in a $5.00 hole than a $5.00 shrub in a 50c hole", still holds good, even though there are perhaps no more 50c shrubs. Do not stint on size or on the quality of the preparation. Now is the time to provide fertility for many years to come.

Organic matter placed under a shrub or tree now may be feeding it fifty years from now. Organic matter breaks down into humus, which slowly disintegrates, releasing about 2% of its nitrogen content a year. Thus if conditions are favorable for growth, a liberal use of compost, well-rotted manure, sewage sludge or similar organic matter may be feeding that specimen half a century from now.

The planting of balled and burlapped specimens of evergreens, shrubs and trees in large holes, particularly if in deep fill that may not be fully settled, does present a problem. Such specimens tend to settle a little if the soil is too loose. This tendency can be overcome by using a firm hard rock, such as a granite boulder, in the bottom of the hole. This should be buried just deep enough so that when the balled specimen is set on it, the planting line on the stem is just where it should be. This rock will keep the evergreen, tree or shrub from settling lower. Also, it allows for filling around the ball with rich soil, which can be settled into place with water, without danger of the ball also settling.

All plants should be set about an inch deeper than they stood in the nursery. The ring of dirt around the trunk or stem will show how deep to set it. Do not, however fill in this extra inch with soil. Instead, leave a shallow basin to trap water. This basin should be filled at intervals and the soil kept moist but not soggy until the new specimen takes hold.

Fertilizer is not too important at this stage if the soil is reasonably rich. Until a woody plant has time to produce new roots, it takes up little plant food from the soil. However, as soon as it shows by throwing out new shoots that it is in active growth a regular feeding program should be started.

Always mulch newly planted stock to reduce evaporation from the soil. A preparation of latex called Wilt pruf can be sprayed over a newly set woody plant to reduce loss of moisture through leaves and bark. Follow directions carefully.

Changes in landscaping — Do not become discouraged if at first the general effect is not as was originally pictured. Time is needed to produce a finished landscape picture. However, even the best-drawn plans

One of the most useful gadgets for laying out curves is the garden hose

sometimes fail to develop according to original impressions. Do not be afraid to make changes, but do so only after considering every possibility without moving existing plants. For example, a striking blue spruce may be too prominent, yet by planting lower growing junipers or yews around it, their contrasting foliage and form may soften its effect without going to the trouble of moving it. If consideration is given to final size and habit, very little renovation should be needed, but if forest type trees are planted,

just because they were cheap originally, it may cost more to move them later than was saved in original cost.

Remaking an old planting—Many of the same advantages can be had if a complete rebuilding of a property is being considered. Since lawns, shrubbery and flower borders will be destroyed during reconstruction, now is the time to make major changes in grade, soil condition and plan.

It is always a temptation to overplant and this is what happens in a few years time.

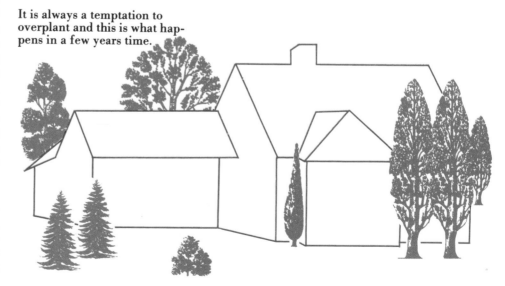

16

LAWNS, TREES & FLOWERS

LAWNS, TREES & FLOWERS

A rich green lawn adds beauty to any home

All about lawns

Lawns—Just as soon as the grading has been completed on the property, the first thing that should be done is to surround the house with lawns as soon as possible.

For the average size city and suburban garden we try to keep both the front and back lawn free of shrubs and trees, except for the sides, the rear of the property and the foundation planting surrounding the house. There is no point in crowding the lawn with specimen shrubs and trees be-

cause this will make mowing very difficult and the overall effect would be cluttered and unsightly. Of course, this rule would not apply to large properties an acre or more in size.

Value of a Lawn—Think of some of the attractive gardens you've seen the past few years and I'm sure that the one landscape feature that stands out in your memory is the beautiful lawn surrounding each of them. A smooth, thick green lawn will materially add to the appearance of any property whether it be a small cottage or a large estate. The beauty of flower beds, trees and shrubs can be half spoiled by a rough brown lawn.

Lawns are becoming more and more important with the modern trend to out-door living. Usually part of the lawn, either behind or to the side of the property can be divided into a living out area and a play area for the children. It's a good plan to separate the two areas by a low hedge or a flower border. No sense putting in a make-shift lawn here. Such lawn areas will have to be able to take plenty of rough treatment. If there is a level area and one with a slope, make the sloping part the children's play area. Recreation authorities will tell you that children get far more fun from rolling down grass banks than almost any other single activity.

Shall I sow seed or lay sod — In making a new lawn we are faced with the somewhat difficult question of whether to sow seed or sod. Until recently there was only one real answer to such a question and that was to sow seed. We now have qualified men who are growing quality nursery sod which will give you a good lawn. Formerly all the sod used for lawns came from along the highways and byways and was nothing but old pasture sod almost useless for lawn purposes. No doubt about it, sod will give you a quick lawn but it is more expensive than sowing seed. For most people the answer to a fine lawn is to sow seed. If you do use sod make sure you know its source and if it isn't especially grown for lawn purposes don't buy it.

Best time to sow a new lawn — No doubt about it the best time to sow a new lawn is in the Fall. For many families moving into a new home in the spring it would be impossible for them to wait until fall. You can expect good success from spring sowing provided you make your preparations carefully. Be ready to sow seed just as soon as the soil is workable in the Spring. Order your supplies of seed, humus and fertilizer 2 or 3 weeks ahead of the time they will be needed.

Buying a new property—If you are buying a new property, preparations for the lawn start before the building of the house. Where there are some trees already on the property, decide on the location of your house and what trees are to be saved. Then, build a protective guard around them. Next have four to six inches of topsoil bulldozed from the entire lot area and saved in a corner for replacement over the lawn after you have finished building. It's important to save this topsoil because it contains organic matter, bacteria and plant food which will go a long way toward producing a better lawn.

Preparation of the soil — It's quite possible that for one reason or another you may have to work with the soil you have. Poorer soil if well drained can be made to produce a good lawn if you take care to use correct soil preparation, lots of humus and fertilizer, and the right kind of grass seed. Since the soil is poor you will need to use plenty of humus and fertilizer every year for quite some time. In turn, the grass will gradually produce enough organic matter to change the poor soil into reasonable topsoil.

Regardless of whether your soils are heavy or light the treatment is the same as far as adding humus is concerned. Light sandy soils, as we mentioned before, are composed of comparatively big pieces of rock which do a poor job of holding moisture and plant food materials. To improve them we add a quantity of humus to the soil which will act like a sponge to hold onto the moisture and plant food. You can improve sandy soils still more by adding two inches of heavier soil at the same time you work in the humus.

Heavy clay soils are always poorly drained and they shrink and crack open when they dry out. Such soils are composed of very tiny particles of soil which pack tightly together and do not allow enough air to circulate for good root growth. Heavy traffic in the living out or play areas will pack a clay soil tighter than ever. The only way to improve these heavier soils is to add

The lawn, trees and foundation planting help give the house a look of permanence

lots of humus.

What kind of humus to use—There are several forms of humus available. The one to use should be the handiest and the cheapest. Good results can be had by using any one of the following: material processed from sewage, peat moss, leaf mould or compost. The use of well rotted barnyard manure or discarded mushroom manure is not recommended because these usually contain numerous weed seeds which will germinate and come back to haunt you over a period of years.

Apply the humus at the rate of five or six bushels per hundred square feet provided your soil was reasonable farm land or topsoil in the beginning. In the case of subsoils it will pay to step up the amount of humus used to eight to ten bushels per hundred square feet. Where peat moss is used, three of the jumbo bales per thousand square feet will be enough where the soil is reasonably good. Step it up to four bales in the case of subsoils.

Use of complete fertilizer or plant food—At the same time as you apply the humus scatter a complete fertilizer or plant food over the soil at the rate of four pounds per hundred square feet or forty pounds per thousand square feet.

Best way of applying fertilizer—The best and the easiest way of applying the fertilizer evenly is to use a fertilizer spreader. In buying one of these don't count your pennies and buy the cheapest machine available. You will be using your spreader for many years so you'll want one which will stand up to considerable use and hard work. Fertilizer spreaders can be set so that they will spread the plant food at a given rate per hundred square feet. Furthermore, if you buy one of the better models, you will be able to use it for sowing the grass seed as well.

Working the humus and fertilizer into the soil—The best way of working the humus and complete fertilizer into the soil is with a rotary tiller. If you check the classified advertisements of your daily newspaper you will no doubt see that the services of a man, who does custom roto tilling, are available at so much an hour. Not only will the rotary tiller thoroughly mix the soil, humus and fertilizer together, but will leave the soil in a flour-like condition, ideal for the final grading and raking.

The final preparation of the seed bed —The final preparation of the seed bed is most important. The area will need raking several times, coupled with a final rolling so

19

as to achieve a fine level seed bed. While raking make sure your grade is level and free of bumps. If you don't take out the bumps now you won't be able to once the lawn becomes well established. Levelling before you sow the seed may take a few extra hours, but it will pay dividends in the form of a lawn that not only looks better but is easier to manage. At seed time there should be no lumps on the surface of the soil larger than a grain of wheat and most of the soil should be the same texture as flour.

Water well before sowing seed — Newly graded soil should be well settled before sowing grass seed. One of the best ways of doing this is to give it a good watering. Make sure the spray is fine enough so it won't disturb the soil. Such a watering will also help to show up any depressions or low areas. Be sure and fill these in before starting to sow seed.

Choosing the right grass seed mixture—It's been my experience that it pays to buy the best grass seed mixture available.

A first class grass seed mixture should contain at least 60% Kentucky or Merion Bluegrass. You will need three lbs. per thousand square feet of lawn area if you use a first class mixture whereas you'll need five lbs. per thousand square feet of the so-called cheaper mixtures. In the end the cheaper kinds can be just as expensive or even more so because you need almost twice as much seed.

White clover is not for you—White clover is unfortunately used in many of the cheaper grass seed mixtures. In still other cases people request that it be added to the mixture mainly because it will stay greener than most grasses during hot dry periods. Despite this advantage there is no place for white clover in a good lawn.

Clover is a legume and as such has the ability to take the free nitrogen of the air and transform this into plant food. This means that the clover soon takes over from the other grasses especially if a regular feeding programme is not carried out.

White clover is coarse in texture and forms patches that give the lawn a spotty appearance. It's soft and slippery and can really cause the best grass stains you've ever seen. In winter the clover patches are bare and these turn to mud spots in the early spring. The best advice that I can give you is not to use it.

Which shall I use, Kentucky or Merion Bluegrass — For many years Kentucky blue grass has reigned supreme as the best lawn-grass in Canada and the United States. It spreads well by means of underground stems called rhizomes. Under favourable conditions these underground stems renew the turf, providing the dense, close-knit cover desired.

However, Kentucky Bluegrass does have certain failings and limitations. Leaf-spot disease often thins the turf. Then it may be infested with crabgrass and other weeds in the hot summer months when bluegrass is semi-dormant and unable to resist invasion. On top of this, most home gardeners want to mow their lawns closer than is best for Kentucky bluegrass. They prefer close mowing because they are indulging more and more in outdoor activities such as badminton, croquet and lawn tennis. This has also meant the need for a bluegrass that is heat and drought resistant and able to withstand wear and tear during the hot summer months.

Merion Bluegrass has over 2 million seeds per pound whereas rye grass has only 300,000 or approximately one seventh of that amount per pound. Because of the plant's vigorous sodding characteristics a light seeding of 2 lbs. per 1,000 square feet will produce a good turf instead of the usual recommendation of 5 lbs. per 1,000 square feet.

Merion has a broader leaf than either Kentucky Bluegrass or bent. To some people this has meant that it is not as attractive. On the other hand, the broad leaf combined with thick growth makes a resilient and more uniformly cushioned turf.

In my own garden I have found that Merion is much darker in colour than other grasses. At the same time though, it must be

It pays to buy the best grass seed mixture available

admitted that Merion Bluegrass needs more fertilizer and more care to keep it looking its best. The leaf growth is slower and this means that less mowing is required.

An outstanding feature of this new grass is its deep rooting characteristic. No other fine lawn grass has such deep roots. The roots reach down to deeper soil for water and are able to get it when most other lawn grasses, with shorter roots, begin to turn brown from lack of water.

The grass is relatively slow to start and requires patience and care in its first stages of growth. I think it is also true to say that the results later on more than compensate for this. When planting straight Merion you must allow for a germination period of anywhere from 15 to 28 days. This will give the weeds a chance to get started and compete the first summer. By late Fall most weeds will be crowded out by Merion or they can be eliminated by weed killers. Although many accepted authorities recommend that Merion be seeded alone for best results, there are some who prefer a finer silkier textured turf than is provided by a straight Merion lawn. They feel that the mixtures help allow for moisture, fertility, and soil conditions too varying for any one grass, no matter how good, to completely master. Then too, when lawns are planted in the Spring other grasses in such a mixture will produce an earlier greening and more rapid early growth. It is important to realise that any mixture should contain at least 40% Merion Bluegrass to be effective.

Sowing the seed — Seeding must be done evenly or there will not only be an uneven pattern to the grass, but there will be bare spots. Your fertilizer spreader or cyclone seeder is the best way of making sure the seed is sown evenly. Divide the seed in half and sow one part one way and the other at right angles to it.

After the seed is sown rake the soil lightly using the tips of the rake teeth making sure you only cover the seed about one eighth of an inch deep. If you cover the seed much deeper than that it will not grow.

Care after seeding—Right after the seed has been sown is the time to roll the lawn with an empty roller to firm the ground against footprints. Do this when the ground is not wet so that the soil and the seed will not stick to the roller. The lawn will need watering within 24 hours of this final rolling. Seed must be wet before it can germinate. You may worry when you see many birds eating the lawn seed. Don't worry. The amount of seed they eat is seldom important. The first sprinkling must be thorough, but gentle to avoid washing the soil away. Try and water from the sides rather than dragging the hose across the freshly sown seed. It's important to keep the seed bed moist until the grass is well started or the entire lawn may be lost.

If there was no rye or red top in your seed mixture, seedlings may not appear for ten days or even more. Don't get alarmed. Your neighbour with a poor seed mixture will get a quicker lawn but it won't last. You can be certain your lawn will be better in the end.

When to make the first mowing— It's most important to have the blades of your lawn mower sharp when it comes time to make the first mowing. Have the mower set so that it will cut the grass two inches high. Wait until the grass is three inches high before doing this first mowing. Actually there is no reason to cut the grass any shorter than two inches at any time, but you can cut a Merion lawn to one and a half inches if you so desire.

Merion bluegrass keeps its dark green color even in hot weather

21

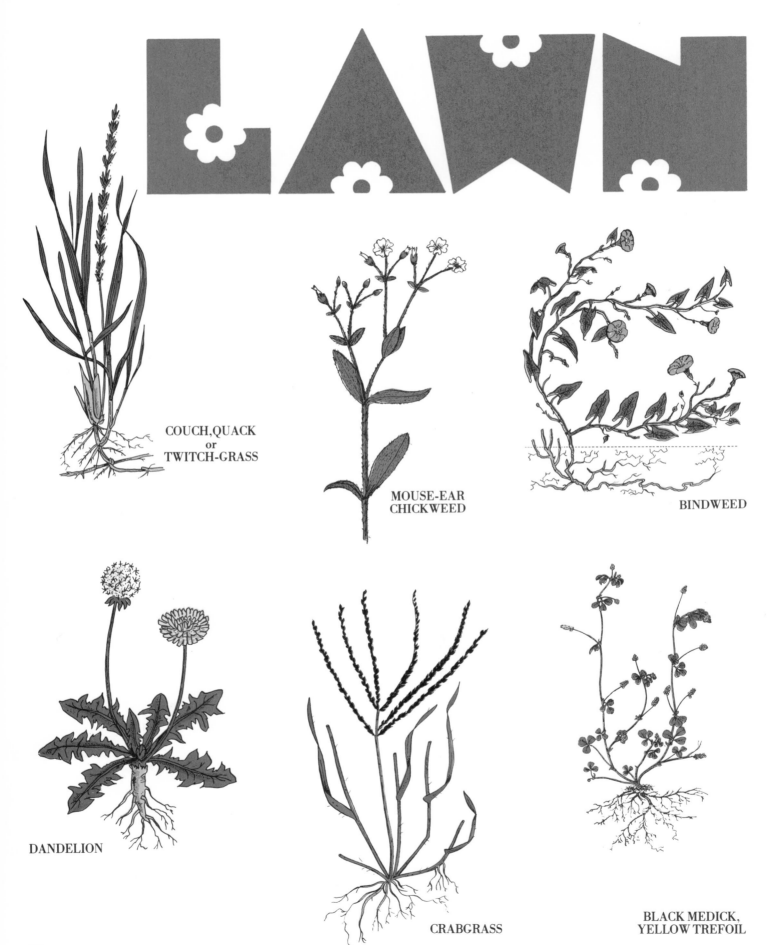

LAWN

COUCH, QUACK
or
TWITCH-GRASS

MOUSE-EAR
CHICKWEED

BINDWEED

DANDELION

CRABGRASS

BLACK MEDICK,
YELLOW TREFOIL

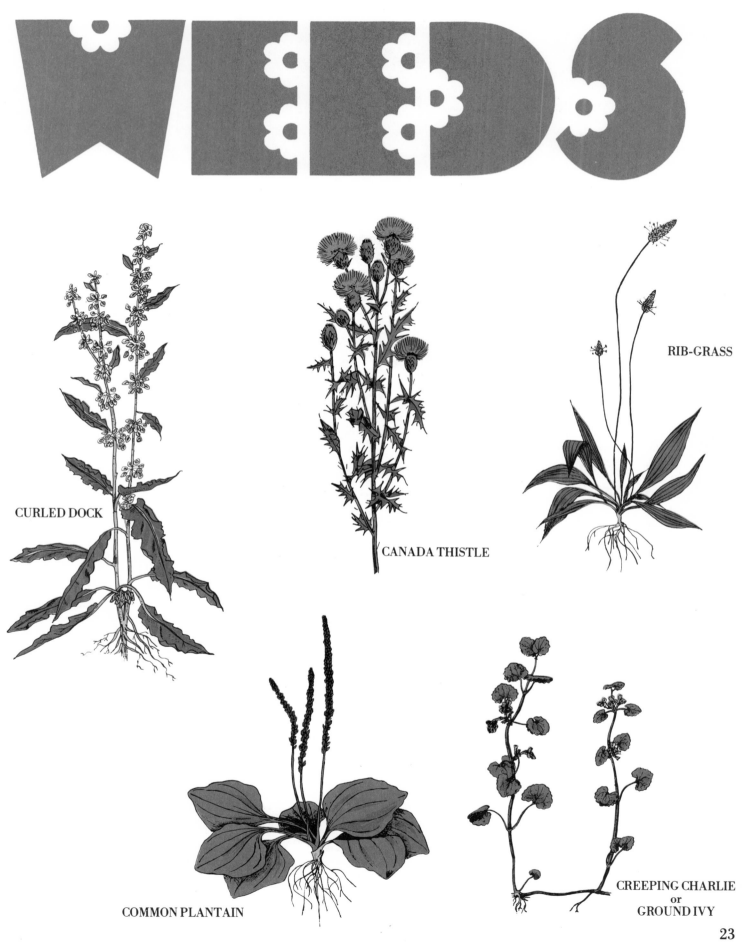

WEEDS

CURLED DOCK

CANADA THISTLE

RIB-GRASS

COMMON PLANTAIN

CREEPING CHARLIE
or
GROUND IVY

Shade trees add beauty and privacy to a property

All about trees

SHADE TREES — In making plans to plant shade and flowering trees, we should remember there is no greater natural asset to a property. They add beauty, form windbreaks, give shade, privacy and an extensive variety of color. On top of all this they add considerable value to the house and property.

In choosing shade and flowering trees for the garden we need to select varieties that are known to be hardy and will be in proportion to the size of your house and lot.

Size — Some of the worst mistakes in landscaping are made when final size of a plant is not known and it is misused. One such mistake, repeated hundreds of thousands of times throughout North America, is the use of a pair of Colorado blue spruces, one on each side of the front door of a modest home. Beautiful at first, these grow to be veritable monsters, hiding and obscuring the house they are supposed to adorn. Almost as bad are the Virginia Red Cedars, sold widely because they are cheap, and are also used to accent house entries.

All plantings should be in scale. Never use a forest tree when a small species such as the hawthorn or flowering crab is indicated. Formerly, this mistake was not as conspicuous as it is today; in the days of two and three story homes, few trees would grow tall enough in one lifetime to over-power them. Today, the modern ranch house or flat top is lost under a towering sycamore or oak in a few years. Many old-time nurseries made the mistake of continuing to propagate trees in scale with two and three story homes and are still promoting their sale. Be sure before selecting a shade tree or shrub that it is in keeping with the house it is to ornament.

Any tree that you do plant should have a purpose. You may want to plant it for shade; to screen out an unsightly view; or to provide a beautiful scene through a window. It is important not to overload with too many trees of the one variety, or to plant so many trees that once they have put on a little height they will screen out the sun altogether.

Generally speaking the best plan is to keep most trees to the sides and the rear of the property. It is a good plan to look out through the windows of your house when selecting choice locations for trees. By doing this you will be able to choose planting sites that not only provide garden beauty, but frame or add to the view as seen from indoors.

Location — Any trees that are planted near the house should be kept approximately 25′ from it. Other good locations are to the back and sides of the property; near the street line; on the edges of the lawn area; and near the patio and children's play area.

In all but the colder areas planting time will be either early in the Spring, just as soon as the soil is workable, or in the Fall. If possible, try and buy trees that are from 8 to 12 feet in height. Also, try and select a thick-headed tree with a straight trunk and a heavy root system.

Air conditioning with shade trees— Not many beginners to gardening realize that the garden and home can be air-conditioned to a large extent by shade trees. Certainly the hot summer sun can make things very uncomfortable without adequate shade.

In planning planting sites for shade trees you want to choose a location which will give the garden or the house all kinds of protection from the sun. Locate the trees some distance from the part that you want shaded, slightly north of due west. If you plant the trees right over the spot the shade will fall to the east of it in the afternoon. The hottest part of the summer day is usually in mid and late afternoon when the sun's rays slant considerably. To get around this, plant far enough West so that the tree will be able to intercept the slanted rays and the shade will fall on the desired area.

For shade directly over outdoor living areas at mid-day the tree should be planted at the edge of the area, but not where an outdoor barbecue or fireplace will be able to scorch the leaves on the lower branches.

The same rules will hold true for shading of terrace or patio. If the terrace is on the east side of the house, only the directly overhead sun needs to be screened off because the house will shade the terrace in the afternoon. In this case the shade tree is placed right beside the patio or terrace to guard against the mid-day sun. But if the patio is on the west side of the house, you may need two trees, one at some distance to the west to block the hot afternoon sun, and one close to the patio to intercept the sun's rays at mid-day and up to the middle of the afternoon.

Is the effort worthwhile? There is little doubt that shade trees can make a difference of four to ten degrees in the temperature of the outdoor living area. This can mean the difference on a hot summer day between comfort and discomfort. Correctly located shade trees also help to eliminate the harsh glare of the sun.

These suggestions for cooling parts of the garden can also be used to make various rooms inside the house more comfortable, by planting trees which will shade the wall of the house and one or more windows, from the hot afternoon sun.

Recommended trees for landscaping the garden—It is only during the past few years that a new group of fast growing shade trees have been developed with few faults. Today there are quite a number of trees that not only grow quickly, but have none of the faults of the so-called weed trees such as the weeping willow, Lombardy and Carolina poplars, Manitoba maple and Chinese elm.

Most of these new trees will grow anywhere from 3 to 5 feet a year once they are established in the garden and provided they are planted in reasonably good soil.

Moraine locust—One of the best of the newer shade trees. Unlike the older locusts this new variety produces neither thorns nor seed pods, yet it grows more rapidly and has a built-in disease resistance. This tree grows at the rate of 3 to 5 feet a year, which means that under reasonable growing conditions, it should be about 25 feet in height in about 10 years. This is considerably faster than what the average tree will do.

The moraine locust is round shaped when young, but grows tall and vase-shaped as it gets older. It makes a worthy substitute for the beautiful elm trees which are now threatened with extinction by the Dutch Elm disease.

Like the common forms of locust, this new tree is extremely tolerant of smoke, soot and dust which makes it ideal for city conditions. Foliage is dark green, and the leaves are so fine and lace-like and crumble so quickly that raking them in the Fall is unnecessary.

At maturity it will be around 40 feet in height.

The fast growing sunburst locust

Sunburst thornless locust—The most spectacular introduction in ornamental shade trees in the past few years is the Sunburst Thornless Locust. Again we have another fast-growing tree with few if any faults. The tips of the branches are a bright golden yellow, shading to bronze at the ends, and appear as if you have taken a paint brush and covered the tips of each branch with bright gold paint.

The inner branches have a rich, green foliage and when this is contrasted with the golden colored ends of the outer branches, it makes it look just like a flowering tree bursting into bloom.

Being a hardwood, it is not easily broken down in Winter wind and ice storms which regularly ravage soft wooded trees such as willows, poplars and Manitoba maples.

The sunburst locust has a beautiful pyramidal branching habit. The leaves are so small that they fall between the grass plants and do not need to be raked up. This tree has been found to be extremely hardy in test plantings all over the country. It makes an excellent lawn specimen shade tree, because the diameter of the trunk is very small in relation to other trees of a similar height. At maturity 30 to 40 feet.

Moraine ash — Here we have another fine new tree which should not be confused with the ordinary ash. Special breeding and selections have eliminated all of the older undesirable features, making it an ideal tree for lawn or street planting.

The new moraine ash has a very attractive symmetrical shape and bears small olive-green leaves which persist later in the Autumn than those of the ordinary ash trees.

When they do fall, they sift through the lawn grasses and do not need raking up.

This fine new tree also has an attractive smooth bark which adds to its cleanliness and desirability. It will thrive under a wide variety of soil conditions.

At full maturity it will be 35 to 40 feet in height.

Red chestnut — In choosing an attractive shade tree for the garden, one of the trees you cannot afford to overlook is the red horsechestnut. Everyone knows the glorious array of white bloom that the ordinary chestnut produces, but just imagine the same tree with red flowers. It is a fairly fast-growing shade tree which is incredibly beautiful when in bloom. Flowering time is May and June and unlike the common chestnut, this tree does not bear nuts and so is very clean. Grows to approximately 30 feet.

Pin oak — Most oak trees are slow growers, but the stately pin oak is the exception to the rule and is one of the fastest growing of the oak family. The foliage is rich green, deeply cut and becomes a glossy

25

copper color in the late Fall. It is one of the few trees that are generally disease and insect free. Everyone likes its symmetrical, pyramidal form. At maturity it stands 30 to 40 feet high.

Mountain ash—One of the most popular of the smaller shade trees. It is a very ornamental tree of moderate growth which makes an ideal lawn specimen. In the Spring large flat clusters of white flowers are produced followed by huge bunches of flashy orange-red berries. These can be a big factor in attracting birds to the garden. It grows to a height of 18 to 25 feet with a maximum spread of 15 feet.

Little leaf linden — Here we have an ideal shade tree for the home garden, and one of the very best trees for street planting, as it is able to withstand the fumes, smoke and dust better than most trees. The trees are very long lived, have a dense pyramidal shape, have handsome heart-shaped foliage, and grow to 100 feet.

Weeping mulberry—One of the finest of the small lawn specimen trees which only grows 6 feet high. It is sometimes called the "umbrella tree' and has long weeping branches which grown up to 5 feet in length. The fruits are tasty and edible and are attractive not only to human beings, but also to birds.

Norway maple — A stately round-headed tree capable of withstanding smoke, soot and other adverse growing conditions. Has been long recognized as one of the choicest shade trees. Leaves are dark green and very dense all over the tree. In the Fall they turn a rich yellow and orange to create an impressive sight.

Trees grow 50 to 60 feet high when fully grown.

Harlequin maple—This is a new variegated leaf Norway maple. Try and visualize a tree completely covered with variegated silver green leaves. The center of the leaf is a rich green, the outside edge is silver-white. It is a moderately rapidly growing tree which develops a lovely round head. It is a rare tree seldom seen in gardens, yet is perfect for shade on the lawn.

At maturity it will be approximately 40 feet tall.

Pyramidal oak — This striking vertical

Pin oak is one of the fastest growing of the oak family

Mountain Ash is one of the most popular of the smaller shade trees.

oak tree grows in somewhat the same shape as the lombardy poplar, but has none of its faults. A lombardy poplar tends to grow very fast until it is about 20 years old, and then gradually but surely dies away. The pyramidal oak is more compact, slower growing and lives for a great many years. The dark brown leaves cling to the branches until early Spring and give the tree a most attractive Winter appearance. During the growing season the fine green foliage is a joy to behold.

Schwedler maple—During the past two decades the Schwedler maple has become a very popular shade tree. In the early Summer it has reddish purple foliage which changes to green towards the end of June. This maple is hard wooded and has a good branching habit. It needs to be planted to the sides or rear of the property as it grows 30 to 50 feet in height.

Japanese red maple — This is a rare and colorful dwarf tree growing approximately 6 feet, sometimes used as a small shrub. Because of its slow growth it makes an excellent specimen tree or shrub for the lawn. Its foliage is never dense enough to harm the lawn and its brilliant crimson foliage never fails to attract attention. Having leaves blood red in color there is nothing better for contrasting among the evergreens in the foundation planting or in the shrub border. The Japanese maple does best when planted in full sun but will tolerate moderate shade. Under shady conditions the crimson color is not nearly so pronounced.

White birch — One of the best ways of using the beautiful white silver birch trees around the garden, is to plant them in clumps of three. Granted, a single tree is also very attractive, but a clump of three seems to add much more charm to the garden. The growth of the white birch is gracefully upright. Even in the Winter the delicate branches make a lovely silhouette against the drab colors of the other trees in the background.

It is best not to start with trees that are too large. If well fed and watered, birches are fast growers, considering the fact that they are a hardwood. Eventually they will grow 35 to 40 feet in height; so do not plant them underneath or close to public utility wires.

Do not be disappointed if the bark of your birch trees is not always white, be-

The white birch is gracefully upright

cause often they do not reach this color until they are about four years old. At this time a chemical change takes place enabling the bark to become white.

You can create some wonderful effects in your garden, by placing a flower bed around a clump of birches.

In all too many cases, most people use them merely as a lawn specimen. This is a mistake, because by placing a large flower bed at the base of the clump of these white silver birches your garden can come alive with a beauty not usually seen in the garden world.

FLOWERING SHADE TREES

One of the most important features of any landscape plan should be the use of flowering shade trees, because nothing will add more beauty, charm and distinctiveness to the house and garden. Indeed, many of them seem to have been specially designed for the smaller gardens because they do not grow very tall, or cover a large area at maturity. The average height of most of the flowering shade trees would be around 15 feet.

These are good trees to locate where they can be seen from windows or alongside patios and living-out areas. Many of them are small enough that they can be spotted along the boundaries of the property, and yet will not compete with nearby beds and borders.

Most of the flowering shade trees also

make excellent lawn specimen trees because they do not cover too large an area and will permit a lawn to be established around them.

Recommended varieties—The various flowering crab apples are among the best of the flowering shade trees. They not only provide a tremendous display of bloom in late May and early June, but after the flowers fade they remain an attractive shade tree, with bronze colored foliage.

As the Summer begins to fade away, they become covered with attractive fruits, many of which are edible.

Flowering crab apples can be grown in either shrub or tree form, so when ordering them from your local nursery or garden center, be sure to specify whether you want the tree or the shrub form.

Almey crab—One of the most beautiful of all flowering crab apples, producing masses of huge flowers which are a fiery crimson in color. White markings at the base of each petal give the effect of a five-sided star. Almey grows 12 to 15 feet in height at maturity.

The Strathmore crab has a pyramidal form

Crab apples are among the most beautiful flowering trees

Strathmore crab—A new type of pyramidal flowering crab which features glorious blossoms and handsome foliage. In early Spring you will enjoy its masses of rosy pink blossoms that literally cover the tree from top to bottom. When not in bloom the naturally ascending branches are covered with large, reddish bronze leaves that in the Fall turn to shades of brilliant orange and scarlet, accented with hundreds of miniature apples. Strathmore grows 10 to 15 feet tall in a slim symetrical column, tapering to a point at the top.

Dolgo crab — Produces masses of wonderful flowers, followed by an equal number of bright red fruits which are unsurpassed for jellies and preserving.

Aldenhamensis — Wine purple red flowers are semi-double. The foliage is a bronze color.

Amisk—Early flowering with very ornamental fruit (not good for cooking). Flower is an amaranth pink with darker veins. Small rose-hip-like fruits are just as beautiful as the flowers, lasting late into the Fall.

Geneva — A dual purpose variety which bears large dark red bloom followed by lovely large dark red apples.

Makamik — This variety blooms every year when all others have finished. Its color is a deep rosy red with darker veins

27

and produces a big crop of flowers every year.

Simcoe is a lovely rose pink with reddish bronze foliage.

Sisipuk — Here we have another very late bloomer, thus prolonging the flowering season. The attractive flowers are rose colored with a white center. The ox-blood red fruits are ¾ of an inch in diameter, hang on all Winter, but are not good for cooking.

Van Essenstine is one of the best varieties of flowering crab apples. The growth is upright, clean, and the foliage is a glossy, light green in color. Flowers are a double pink, being a dark pink on the reverse side, and light pink as the petals open on the inside.

FLOWERING CHERRIES

Kwanzan—This is the spectacular flowering cherry that makes such a wonderful show every year around Washington, D.C. Trees bloom a year or two after transplanting, and grow anywhere from 20 to 30 feet tall. Double bright rose-pink flowers completely clothe the branches in early Spring. It is not hardy in all areas, so check with your local nursery or garden club before you buy.

Hisakura is one of the finer dwarf trees, and is the hardiest of all the Japanese flowering cherries. This variety grows 15 feet tall, and makes an especially good lawn

Hundreds of blooms are produced every year on a flowering cherry

specimen tree. The branches are simply smothered with double pink flowers every Spring.

Paul's Scarlet Hawthorn

This is the old-fashioned flowering tree that our parents knew and loved. This is not surprising because this exceptionally fine flowering tree produces extra large quantities of double, deep crimson scarlet flowers, having rich green foliage which makes a wonderful background to highlight the flowers. Its long flowering period and attractive appearance after flowering makes this variety one of the best lawn specimen trees. Grows 20 feet high.

Nothing equals a scarlet hawthorn in bloom

Magnolia

There is little doubt that the magnolias are one of the most elegant of all the flowering trees. Before the leaves appear, the trees are covered with a mass of fragrant, huge tulip-shaped flowers. These are colored a rosy-white on the inside, and a lively pink color on the outside. Leathery, deep green, waxy foliage follows the flowers and provides a restful mass of cool green during the remainder of the growing season.

White flowering dogwood — This is one of the most beautiful of our native flowering trees. Here is a superb lawn specimen tree for areas where the Winters are not too cold. It grows well in partial shade and is literally covered with large white blossoms early in the Spring. The flowering dogwood has a very long flowering period of anywhere from 3 to 5 weeks. In the Fall it again puts on a magnificent display with the foliage turning to brilliant shades

of red, and at the same time the branches are covered with red berries. Trees grow 10 to 12 feet in height.

Red flowering dogwood — Everyone should know this lovely artistic flowering tree. It produces a great profusion of large rose-red flowers in the Spring, and glossy red berries in the Fall. There are many locations in the garden where it may be planted, not only because of the exquisite red color of the flowers, fruits and leaves, but because of its attractive and unique branching habit. At full maturity it grows to 12 feet in height.

Golden rain tree — One of the best medium size flowering trees in cultivation. In mid-summer the whole tree is a cascade of golden bloom. Golden yellow flowers are borne in long chains which creates a breathtaking sight when they stir in the breeze. Used as a specimen lawn tree, it will delight both you and your neigbours. Grows 30 feet high.

Red bud — This small tree presents a striking picture, with its clusters of rose-pink flowers in the Spring. These are followed by large heart-shaped green leaves. It is very effective for group plantings in corners of the garden or the shrub border. A redbud tree and a bed of yellow violas planted at its base are one of the most beautiful sights in the early Spring. Matures between 15 and 20 feet.

The golden rain tree makes a delightful lawn specimen tree

The golden chain tree can be grown in either shrub or tree form

Golden chain tree — Here is another dual-purpose tree which can be grown in either shrub or tree form. In June, the bright golden yellow flowers are produced in long hanging clusters 18 to 20 inches in length, closely resembling the blooms of the wisteria. This fairly rare dwarf tree has green bark and foliage, and usually flowers the first year after planting. It is not hardy in colder areas, so check before you plant. Height is 8 to 10 feet.

Purple-leaf plum is one of the finest hardy, small flowering trees for the garden. The flowers are blush pink and are borne in great profusion in the Spring. As they fade, the purple leaves break out on the branches, and keep their color throughout the Summer. The purple leaf plum makes an excellent contrast when planted among or in front of trees having the usual green foliage. It also makes an excellent lawn specimen tree. The maximum height is 15 feet.

Landscaping uses of shade & flowering trees

Recommended trees to provide shade

Norway maple	White birch
Crimson King maple	Red oak
Schwedler maple	Pin oak
Sugar maple	Mountain ash
Moraine locust	Little leaf linden
Sunburst locust	Moraine ash
	Pyramidal oak

Recommended flowering trees

Flowering crab apple	Laburnum
Red horse chestnut	Saucer magnolia
Pauls scarlet hawthorn	Star magnolia
Flowering dogwood	Flowering cherry

Recommended weeping trees

Cutleaf weeping birch	Weeping mulberry
	Weeping cherry

Recommended trees for Autumn color

Red maple	Flowering dogwood
Sugar maple	Red oak
Katsura tree	Pin oak

Recommended trees for city conditions

Norway maple	Carolina poplar
Northern catalpa	Lombardy poplar
Moraine locust	Little leaf linden
London plane	Chinese elm

Recommended trees with colored foliage in the Summer

Crimson king maple	Purple beech
Schwedler maple	Purple plum
	Purple sand cherry

Quick-growing trees for screening purposes—Note: Not recommended otherwise.

Silver maple	Lombardy poplar
White poplar	Laurel willow
Carolina poplar	Chinese elm

A good location for planting trees is the edge of the lawn area

Add a splash of color when landscaping the garden

Low cost landscaping with annuals, perennials & biennials

One of the easiest and most inexpensive ways for the new home owner to obtain a big splash of color the first year is to create flower borders along the sides and the back of the garden.

In the larger gardens such a border can form the dividing line between the back lawn and the vegetable garden.

The first year you may not be prepared or able to use annuals, biennials and perennials in your borders and will probably want to stick to low-cost annuals.

Many of these can be grown in soil that is not sufficiently prepared for perennials and biennials. The use of annual borders can be looked upon as the preparation for permanent mixed flower borders later on.

The two most important points to keep in mind are the preparation of the soil and the minimum width. There are few annuals that will grow well in soils that contain very

little humus and plant food. You must be prepared to dig large quantities of humus and fertilizer before the soil will be ready for planting.

As far as the width is concerned your border will need to be wide enough to take care of the three main height groups of annuals, perennials and biennials. These are usually divided into three classes; low-growing kinds for the front of the border which vary in height from 2 or 3 inches to 18 inches; medium height varieties which grow anywhere from 18 inches to 2½ feet; and the tallest ones which range from 3 feet to as much as 7 or 8 feet.

To accommodate all of these, your border should have a minimum width of at least six feet, and preferably 8 to 10 feet. It is better to sacrifice some of the lawn area in favor of having enough room in the border.

For the beginner to gardening the easiest thing to do is to have the sides of the border straight. This means easy maintenance the first 2 or 3 years. One thing to avoid at all costs is to have a lot of small scallops or curves down the front of the border. There is no doubt that curves do add a great deal of beauty, but they should be soft and sweeping.

All borders need a suitable background to show the various flowers at their best.

For this we have a choice of several true hedge plants. These have fibrous roots which stay close to the plant and do not reach out into the border to rob the flowers of food and moisture. For most areas privet makes an excellent hedge plant. In the very cold areas where the temperatures fall regularly below zero in the Winter the high bush cranberry is excellent.

A painted wooden fence also is a fine background for any border. One of the important points in its favor is that once erected and painted, there is usually far less maintenance than for a living hedge.

Whichever type you choose make sure that you leave plenty of room for maintenance between the hedge or fence and the flowers. Hedges will have to be pruned, sprayed and fertilized several times each year. Wooden fences need painting and repairing from time to time.

Flowers — On the smaller property, advantage must be taken of every available inch of space if a good show of color is wanted. Drives and walks should be edged with narrow beds in which tulips in Spring and annuals in Summer can be planted for a show of vivid bloom. Because of the limited space available for such plantings, only flowers with clear, bright colors, such as marigolds, zinnias, petunias, tulips and narcissi should be used.

In North America, too little use is made of front yard planting. It is not unusual to drive for miles along city and suburban streets without seeing a single attractive garden in front of a home. Even though back yards may be full of brilliant bloom and well-laid out flower beds, the area along the street is drab and uninteresting.

Even a narrow ribbon of color created by bright annuals along a drive or across the area under a picture window can make a tremendous difference in the attractiveness of a home. Nowadays these need not even be grown at home. Most greenhouse operators and garden centers are able to

30

supply a wide range of bedding plants in full bloom to provide instant glamour. By the judicious use of spring-flowering bulbs for early bloom, followed by bedding plants from the florist and followed by hardy chrysanthemums transplanted into the space when the annuals fade, that ideal of every good gardener—continuous bloom—can be made possible. The chrysanthemums, which can be moved in place even when in full bloom, can be started in a row in the vegetable garden or in back of the garage.

Nor should the back yard be neglected. Try to cram color into every available corner. Do, however, watch color schemes carefully; because most back yards are small, harmony between the various patches of flowers must be watched carefully. Usually it is best to stick to a two or three color combination, such as yellow and red for strong contrasts or pink, blue and lavender for a more subtle display.

Flowering shrubs — Because of the limited space available for bloom, make as much use as possible of flowering trees and shrubs. Pick species with care. Give preference to those that have three seasons of beauty—flowers in Spring, interesting foliage in Summer and Autumn color in Fall. Some shrubs, such as forsythia and witchhazel, can be cut as branches in Winter for forced indoor bloom; these give still another use out of the limited space available.

Feeding birds—A bird feeder, particularly if surrounded by evergreens in which birds nest and by shrubs on whose fruits they feed, will give endless hours of pleasure for the entire family. It should be located so that it will be visible from a window during the Winter; otherwise it will probably be neglected. Shrubby dogwoods, various viburnums, crabs, cherries and mulberries are particularly attractive to many birds. If a fruiting arbor vitae is planted nearby, it may attract that lovely visitor, the cedar waxwing. Government bulletins give a long list of shrubs attractive to birds.

Water gardens—Pools are particularly interesting and require less care per square foot than any other type of garden. One common mistake made with pools is equipping them with a fountain or running water and then expecting water lilies to grow. Water lilies and most other aquatic plants demand still water.

Plant material

So far, little has been said about the ornamental value of plant material; it has been considered largely as part of the "Furniture" of the landscape plan. However, if we were considering only its mass and form (all too often the elements considered by landscape architects) we would miss most of the pleasure to be had from a really good landscape scene. Now is the time to become aware of the fact that trees, shrubs, vines and lesser plants have color, form, size and texture.

Texture — This is an element usually neglected by the amateur. He may plant a shrubbery border or a hedge of a single shrub or evergreen, creating a monotonous wall without interest created by variety.

All borders need a suitable background

Petunias make a fine edging for a patio

31

Pools and water gardens are particularly interesting

Sometimes that monotony is needed, as where a garden is to be used only as a place to relax and rest. Its very lack of interest does not call for attention and so serves a special purpose.

Most home owners, however, need to consider the need for variety and contrast in texture. Study evergreens in particular. Junipers used as a background, unless of an unusually striking color, are soft and blend quietly without making much of a splash in the finished landscape scheme. Thus we might use them where we do not want to call attention to a particular spot, as for example, in "planting out" a public utility pole. They might be used also to frame an exciting view which demanded full attention from the observer.

Pines, on the contrary, have a harsh, brisk texture which calls attention to them. Where a juniper might be used to frame a view filled with many features which demand attention, a pine can be used to frame a spectacular view of the sunset, where no details obtrude, but where the blackness and crispness of the pine needles form a striking contrast with the evening colors.

Study texture and use it; it is one of the basic elements of landscaping.

Color — Not all color is afforded by flowers. Over 500 different shades of green have been recorded in the foliage of plants used in American gardens, ranging from the near-black of Japanese pine needles to the silvery green of certain herbs. Since foliage makes up about 80% of the average landscape picture, with flower representing only about 10%, its importance can be appreciated. Not to be overlooked is the value of fruit color, a particularly important factor in Fall. Autumn color in foliage should be studied carefully. A plant with striking Fall foliage, such as the compact burning bush, euonymus alatus compacta, is worth planting if only for its sensational display of rosy red at that season of the year.

In using color, take advantage of contrast. For example, the brilliant yellow and scarlet colors of maples are all the more brilliant when the tree is silhouetted against the somber green of pines.

One thing to keep in mind when using color is to avoid spotty effects. Alternating contrasting colors one by one gives a jarring note. If, however, trees or shrubs are planted in groups of three to five, the jumpy effect of small masses of color is avoided.

Create variety in your garden

Form — A common sight in certain suburban areas where self-trained "landscapers" maintain home grounds is the appearance of a planting of shrubs sheared to identical cones and balls. Whether the plant happens to be a juniper or a privet, it receives the same treatment. Every plant is forced into a common mould, despite a natural habit quite different from that given it by the maintenance man whose only equipment includes a pair of pruning shears and a shovel.

This is not a condemnation of pruning as such; a certain amount of snipping and cutting is needed to keep woody plants within bounds. However, this should be used not as a means of forcing the plant into unnatural habits, but to take advantage of its natural beauty.

It is important to study the natural form of every tree and shrub used in the landscape plan. Any training or trimming done should be directed to maintaining the plant in that form and to keep it from spreading outside the area alloted to it in the original plan.

Beware of the overuse of vegetable "punctuation marks", the narrow, columnar forms of lombardy poplar, Virginia red cedar and pyramidal arbor vitae. These can be used with care where they fit in, but the sight of a long row of lombardy poplars or similar upright forms against a sunset is anything but pleasant.

Do not be satisfied with looking at only one form or variety of a certain plant. For example, the upright form of the Japanese yew with its broad conical form while an excellent evergreen, is much inferior to the Hatfield yew as a plant for hedges. The latter is a tall, blocky oblong of green, which does not need to be beheaded to form an ideal hedge but fills in right down to the ground. Within this one group of evergreens can be found forms ranging all the way from prostrate, sprawling varieties to narrow pyramidal or columnar types that seem almost like another plant entirely.

Evergreens present no problem of change from season to season but all trees and shrubs that drop their leaves in Winter have two forms to contend with. Sometimes a species that is lovely when in leaf is ugly when the foliage goes in Fall. The opposite is also true; some of the most dramatic effects in landscaping can be created by silhouetting a tree with interesting Winter form against an appropriate background. An example is a beech with its silvery bark planted in front of dark evergreens, or a black walnut against a white building.

Foundation planting should not be drab and uninteresting

Not all color is afforded by flowers

33

FOUNDATION PLANTING

FOUNDATION PLANTING

Foundation plantings soften the harsh architectural lines of a house

Foundation plantings are used to soften the harsh architectural lines of the house, to hide part of the foundation wall and to create beauty for this important area.

For older homes a heavy foundation planting was and is needed to hide the ugly stonework or brick of the foundation walls. In many cases the first floor is at least three feet above the ground, leaving a bare space to be hidden by a mass of shrubbery and evergreens.

The coming of the modern ranch style home has changed many of the concepts of foundation plantings. For homes such as these all that is needed is a few well spaced shrubs, evergreens and small trees to form interesting shapes against a contrasting or harmonizing wall.

In the case of the newer homes we no longer need to bring down the apparent height of the house. Many of them look as though they are part of the surrounding landscape already and need no further tying down.

One of the major problems is to find shrubs, evergreens which are dwarf enough to plant under the well-nigh universal picture window and stay that way, so that the view from the window will not be obscured.

All too many new home owners get carried away, rush out and purchase nursery stock before they have a rough plan prepared and the foundation beds ready for planting.

The direction the house faces governs the selection of plant materials;

House facing South — good selection
"   "   East — good selection
"   "   West — about 60% selection
"   "   North — about 20% selection

Houses that face the north or the west receive considerably less sunshine than those facing east or south. In addition, the prevailing wind in the Winter usually hits northern or western exposures with full force and many otherwise reasonably hardy shrubs and evergreens suffer considerable ill effects.

Whatever you do — do not go out into the woods and dig up some of the native evergreens as they will quickly grow out of proportion.

It is important to consider contrasts. If you have a light colored home, then use dark colored shrubs such as the red barberry, pink spiraea and evergreens such as the Japanese yew etc. For dark colored homes use the light colored evergreens and shrubs. The golden pfitzer is a fine evergreen for this purpose. Hydrangeas, golden philadelphus, and golden privet are typical examples of light colored shrubs.

Also to be taken into consideration is the characteristics or growth habits of the shrubs and evergreens. They need to be considered in terms of the house design.

For example — the pyramidal types are placed at the corners or in front of solid wall areas. The spreading types are the ones to be used in front of, and underneath windows.

Do not plant two dark shrubs or evergreen of different varieties side by side— it is much better to use light and dark together to create contrast.

Overplanting is one of the biggest mistakes made by both beginners to gardening, and by unethical landscape men. In fact, more mistakes are made in creating

The foundation planting should flow beyond and around corners in sweeping curves

a foundation planting than in any other part of the garden.

Most foundation beds are far too small. Usually they consist of an oblong bed about three feet wide along the front and sides of the house. This lack of width is a very serious mistake, because first of all we have to have enough room so that every evergreen can be located at least three feet from the foundation wall. Furthermore, the foundation planting needs to be big enough to hold a representative selection of flowering shrubs, Spring flowering bulbs, biennials such as violas and pansies, Summer annuals and the odd perennial.

Six feet would be the minimum width for a foundation planting, and for most gardens you could go as much as eight to ten feet without the beds being too big.

The foundation planting should not con-

sist of a straight oblong bed, and stop dead at the corners or the end of the house, but should flow beyond and around the corners in sweeping curves. Straight horizontal lines actually emphasize the harsh architectural lines of the house, whereas when curves are used it helps to soften them and blend them into the landscape.

One of the worst faults that can happen in the foundation bed that is too small is the tendency to plant the evergreens too close to the foundation wall. This can actually give an evergreen a "schizophrenic" personality in the Winter. The modern basement pushes considerable heat through the foundation wall, and when evergreens are planted only a foot or so from the wall, the part of the tree next to it thinks that Spring has come. On the other hand, the side whose roots are away from the wall

will still be in the grip of Winter. The heat also dries out the soil, and since evergreens continually give off moisture through their needles, even on days when the temperature falls to zero or lower, they can easily be in serious need of water in the dead of Winter.

There is another, and still more important, reason for not planting too close to the foundation wall. You may not realize it, but on a hot July day, with the sun beating down the heat is radiated back from the wall, resulting in temperatures as high as 175 degrees one or two feet from it. This is only 37 degrees removed from the boiling point of water and it is no wonder that evergreens turn brown and die.

The man who has just bought a new home, or the person who is having trouble with evergreens, should examine the soil carefully where the foundation planting is either located or is planned. All too often, when the builder or plasterer is finished with the house, any refuse left over indoors is pushed out through the front windows or doors and becomes mixed with the soil lying immediately in front of the house.

This refuse is almost invariably full of lime, and if there is one thing that will turn an evergreen brown in no time it is lime. It not only harms evergreens and other plants immediately after planting, but continues to do so for a number of years.

Unless one is sure that the soil around the house is good garden or farm soil, and that it is free from lime and other debris, the best plan is to dig out the existing soil and replace it with a good top soil mixture. To ensure success, the soil already there should be removed to a depth of two feet. This may seem like a lot of work at the time, and the cost seem high, but unless the soil is replaced it probably will cost ten times as much over the succeeding few years.

The height of the window above ground level determines the type of plant to be used. Unattractive foundations can be effectively screened and clothed with plant materials. Plant taller evergreens or shrubs in the background with shorter shrubs (with different colored foliage or flowers) or floribunda roses in front for additional interest and color.

If the masonry work is appealing to the eye, spreading evergreens planted far enough apart to allow walls to show between will add interest.

Shrubs for the foundation planting

The plants you use in the foundation planting can be divided into four main groups:

1. **Corner shrubs** planted at the various corners of the house and garage. For this you would use upright evergreens such as Hick's yew, pyramidal cedar, etc., and tall growing shrubs such as forsythia, beauty bush and hydrangeas.

2. **Entrance shrubs**—With glass windows that extend to the floor it is often difficult to pick out the front entrance of many homes. This is particularly true if the space-saving scheme of using the driveway as an entrance walk is followed. One bad feature of this confusion is that oftentimes delivery men and children cut across the lawn to the front door.

Consider color contrasts between the house and the foundation planting

Do not plant evergreens too close to the wall

The direction the house faces governs the selection of plant materials

Special entrance plantings are needed near the doorway

For this reason some special planting is needed near the door to say "This is where you enter".

Here you would also use upright evergreens such as Hick's yew, Blaauw's blue juniper, or the silver juniper, etc.

As far as the flowering shrubs are concerned you could use the various weigelas, flowering quince, or double mock orange, etc.

Another interesting treatment might call for training a handsome flowering vine such as a climbing rose or clematis up one side of the door, perhaps bringing one branch across like an eyebrow to frame its top. On the other side a quality evergreen such as a spreading yew would balance the vine.

3. **Under the window shrubs** — Here we use the very low-growing evergreens such as Myer's juniper, golden pfitzer juniper, and the silver king juniper, etc.

In choosing shrubs for under the window the red leaf barberry, floribunda roses and hydrangea Hills of Snow are among many available.

4. **Facer shrubs** — These give depth and color to any plantings and help to screen out sections of unattractive foundation walls. They also protect evergreens at entrances and corners from damage by dogs and children.

The following evergreens are excellent facer plants:—dwarf mugho pine, dwarf Japanese yew and the silver king juniper. In the shrubs you could use the red leaf barberry, green barberry, floribunda roses and Blue Mist spirea.

Upright Hick's Yew is attractive against a stone wall

The Mountbatten juniper has steel blue foliage

Blaauw's juniper is an excellent dwarf vase-shaped evergreen

HEDGES

Variety	Color of foliage	Special features	Planting distance apart	Location	Optimum trimmed height
Green barberry	Light green, crimson in Fall	Red berries Fall & Winter	9 in. to 15 in.	Sun or partial shade	18 in. to 30 in.
Red barberry	Maroon red	Red berries in Fall	9 in. to 15 in.	Full sun	18 in. to 30 in.
Blue arctic willow	Blue green	Very graceful (if left un-trimmed)			
Boxwood (Korean)	Light green	Green all year, ideal for low edging	6 in. to 9 in.	Sun or shade	10 in. to 15 in.
Bridal Wreath spiraea	Medium green, light orange in Fall	White flowers very hardy	1 in. to 2 in.	Sun or partial shade	3 ft. to 5 ft.
Peking coton-easter	Dark green glossy leaf surface	Very hardy	12 in. to 18 in.	Sun or partial shade	3 ft. to 6 ft.
Dwarf currant	Dark green	Small yellow flowers, best for heavy shade	9 in. to 15 in.	Sun or shade	18 in. to 30 in.
Honeysuckle (in variety)	Medium green	Pink or red, perfumed flowers, orange or red berries	1 ft. to 2 ft.	Sur or partial shade	3 ft. to 7 ft.
Hick's yew	Dark green, new growth lighter	Trims well, evergreen hedge	9 in. to 15 in.	Sun or shade	2 ft. to 4 ft.
High bush cranberry	Green, Maple leaf shape	White flowers, red berries, very hardy	1 ft to 2 ft.	Sun or partial shade	3 ft. to 8 ft.
Hydrangea P.G.	Light green, planted for flowers	Large white turning to pink conical flowers	2 ft. to 3 ft.	Sun or partial shade	2 ft. to 4 ft. *Leave un-trimmed
Laurel leaf willow	Glossy dark green leaf surface	Fast growing, very hardy	2 ft. to 4 ft.	Sun or partial shade	4 ft. to 12 ft.
Lilac (Persian)	Dark green, best left un-trimmed	Long, light, purple flowers (perfumed)	2 ft. to 3 ft.	Sun or partial shade	4 ft. to 10 ft.
Snowflake mock Orange	Medium green	Double white flower	1 ft. to 2 ft.	Sun or partial shade	3 ft. to 6 ft.
Privet hardy amur river	Glossy green	Small white flower, con-sidered "the best"	9 in. to 15 in.	Sun or partial shade	2 ft. to 5 ft.
Rosa multiflora	Light green	Thorny, fruit for birds	1 ft. to 2 ft.	Full sun	3 ft. to 5 ft.
Floribunda roses	Medium green	Most colorful of all hedges	2 ft. to 3 ft.	Full sun	18 in to 24 in.
Rugosa roses	Medium green	Red or pink, no winter protection	2 ft. to 3 ft.		

Shrubs with 'ALL-SEASON' colorful foliage

Variety	Max. Ht.	Bloom Color	Month of Bloom	Character-istics	Uses
Red leaf barberry	2 ft. to 3 ft.	Small Yellow	May	Dwarf bushy habit	Facer shrub Shrub borders, Hedging
Blue leaf Arctic willow	2 ft.	For foliage color		Blue green leaves, very graceful	Facer shrubs Rockery shrub, Hedging
Burning bush	8 ft.	Brilliant Fall color	June	Bright red in Fall	Specimen shrub
Golden leaf spiraea (Golden ninebark)	6 ft.	Creamy white	May & June	Reddish seed clusters in Fall	Shrub borders, accent plant
Golden mock Orange	3 ft. to 5 ft.	White	June	Fragrant bloom, light yellow leaves, prefers sun	Foundation plantings Shrub borders Excellent contrast
Cut leaf golden elder	6 ft. to 8 ft.	Creamy white	June	Golden yellow leaves, purple berries	Shrub borders
Japanese Maple (Acer)	6 ft.	For foliage color		Crimson foliage, prefers sun	Specimen plant
Purple leaf plum	15 ft.	Pink	May	Leaves purplish red	Specimen or contrast shrub
Russian Olive	20 ft.	Fragrant Small Yellow	June	Long, narrow silvery-green leaves	Specimen shrub, contrast shrub, tall hedge
Silver leaf dogwood	4 ft. to 6 ft.	White	May	Variegated silver green leaf, red bark	Specimen shrub Contrast for shrub border
Purple leaved smoke bush	8 ft.	Purple	July	Dark purple foliage	Specimen shrub, shrub border
Tamarix	6 ft.	Pink or red	July	Fine feathery blue-green foliage	Specimen shrub, shrub border
Flowering crab (shrub form)	8 ft.	Pink or red	May	Reddish-bronze leaves	Specimen shrub, group plantings

Approximate tree growth in ten years

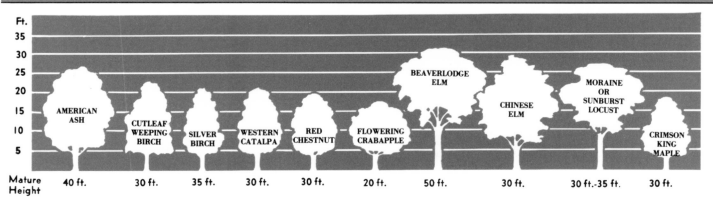

Hardy plants for the 'SHADY LOCATION'

It is a mistake to plant evergreens or shrubs which do not tolerate shade on the north side of a house. Select from those plants listed below.

~Evergreens~

Variety	Color of foliage	Shape	Height at maturity
Hick's yew	Dark green, new growth light green	Columnar, trims well	4 ft to 6 ft.
Dwarf Japanese yew	Dark green, new growth light green	Spreading	2 ft.
*Pfitzer juniper	Light green	Flat spreading	18 in. to 24 in.
*Mugho pine	Medium green	Global, candle-like growth	2 ft. to 3 ft.
*Korean boxwood	Light green	Trims beautifully	18 in to 2 ft.

~Ground covers~

Variety	Color of bloom	Month of Bloom	Shape	Height at maturity
Periwinkle (Vinca)	Blue	May & June	Spreading habit, roots easily	6 in.
Pachysandra (Japanese spurge)	White	June	Light green, shiny leaves	9 in.

~Vines & climbers~

Variety	Color of bloom	Month of Bloom	Special features
*Clematis	White	Aug. to Oct.	Very fragrant
*English ivy	Not apparent		Evergreen, self-clinging
*Boston ivy	Not apparent		Fall color, self-clinging

One of the most frequently asked questions is "How fast does a tree grow?" To help you visualize the "rate of growth" after planting, a chart has been prepared showing the *approximate* size which the various varieties of trees should reach in ten years.

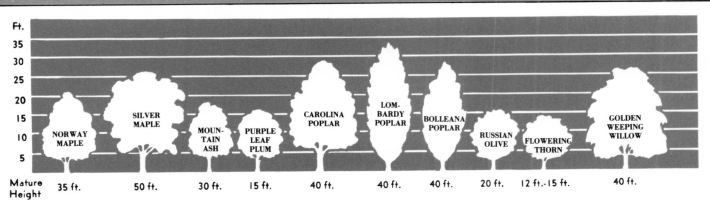

~Deciduous shrubs~

Variety	Color of bloom	Month of Bloom	Special features	Height at maturity
*Green barberry	Small yellowish-white flowers	May	Crimson foliage in Fall, red berries	2 ft. to 3 ft.
Dwarf alpine currant	Small yellow flower	June	Trims well, dark green leaf	2 ft to 4 ft.
*Snowflake mock orange	White flower	June	Sweetly scented	4 ft. to 6 ft.
*Honeysuckle (in variety)	Red or pink flower	May & June	Colored berries	6 ft. to 10 ft.
*Hills of Snow hydrangea Aborescens	White	July & August	Snowball flower	2 ft. to 4 ft.
*Hydrangea P.G.	White to pink	August to Oct.	Cone-shaped flower	3 ft. to 6 ft.
*Hydrangea Nikko Blue	Blue	July & August	Requires acid soil	2 ft.
*Golden flowering currant	Yellow	May & June	Sweet fragrance	4 ft. to 6 ft.
Snowberry	Small rose-colored White	June & July	White berries	3 ft. to 5 ft.
Snowball	flowers	June & July	Large snowball-like flowers	6 ft. to 8 ft.

Height at maturity is the average height when full grown. However most shrubs and evergreens may be trimmed and maintained at lower heights.
*NOTE: Although these plants will grow in full shade, they do better in partial or full sun.

Trees as WINDBREAKS

Variety	Color of foliage	Special features	Planting distance apart	Location	Optimum trimmed height
Chinese elm	Medium green,	Fast growing, trims well	5 ft. to 10 ft.	Full sun	30 ft. Can be trimmed lower
Carolina poplar	Medium green large glossy leaves	Fast growing	15 ft. to 20 ft.	Full sun	40 ft.
Laurel leaf willow	Glossy dark green	Fast growing, grows in most any soil	4 ft. to 6 ft.	Sun or partial shade	30 ft.
Lombardy poplar	Light green	Columnar, fast growing	6 ft. to 10 ft.	Full sun	40 ft.
Silver poplar	Silver-white undersurface of leaves	Columnar, fast growing	6 ft. to 10 ft.	Full sun	40 ft.

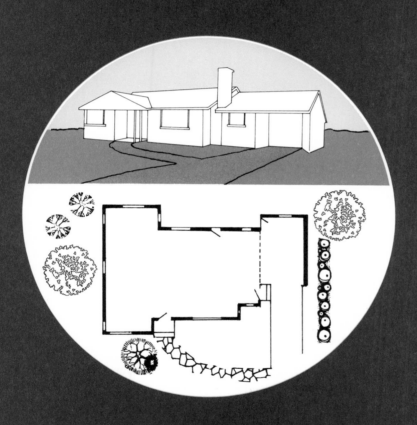

THE PLAN

THE PLAN
A step~by~step landscape plan

"Landscaping" is to change a house on a lot, to a "Home" with individuality and character. The art of "landscaping" is not a difficult one, providing you follow a few simple rules, and prepare an overall plan which can be followed.

You gave considerable thought to plan-ning the inside of your home. The outside deserves equal consideration. It is a mistake to purchase a few trees and shrubs and "stick them in" without considering what the ultimate effect will be. It is much easier to plan now — than to move overgrown material at a later date.

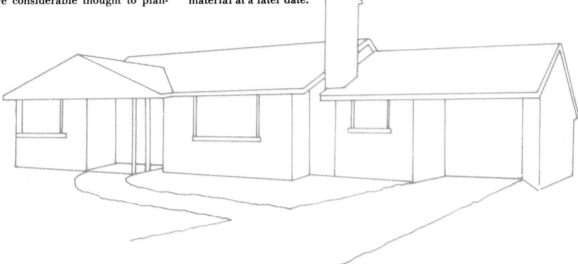

Steps to successful planning

1. Make a drawing to scale of your en-tire property, including the buildings.
2. Designate the four main areas:
(a) Front lawn area (facing the street)
(b) Service area (including children's play-yard)
(c) Fruit and vegetable area (if desired)
(d) Outdoor living room (private area)
3. Locate shade and ornamental trees to receive maximum benefits. Keep in mind tile beds; septic tank, overhead wires and any obstruction above or below the soil. Try to make the trees frame your house, pre-senting a balanced picture, rather than simply planting at random.
4. To obtain the overall desired results, plan each of the areas — (a), (b), (c) and (d) in complete detail. Use ruled graph paper. Each square could equal one foot. Next draw a plan view of the house and plan materials to be used. We suggest you allow 4 to 5 feet for the ultimate spread of the larger flowering shrubs; 3 to 4 feet for the medium growing shrubs and spreading evergreens (such as Pfitzer juniper); 2 to 3 feet spread for such plants as roses; and upright evergreens (e.g. Hick's yew), or global evergreens (e.g. globe cedar); 1 to 2 feet for nearly all perennial plants. This method permits you: (a) to determine the number of plants required; (b) to arrange for the best ultimate results.

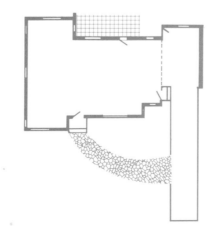

The 'foundation' planting

The plants used around the foundation can be divided into four main groups:
1. Corner shrubs (upright evergreens or tall growing shrubs).
2. Entrance shrubs (upright evergreens or medium growing shrubs).
3. Under the window shrubs (spreading evergreens or low growing shrubs).
4. Facer shrubs (global and spreading evergreens or smaller growing shrubs).

When selecting plant material always consider the ultimate height and shape. Use shrubs at the corners which eventually grow larger than those at the entrance.

BE SURE TO KEEP ALL PLANTS AT LEAST 2 FEET OUT FROM THE FOUNDATION OF THE HOUSE

STEP 1 ~ Corner & entrance plants

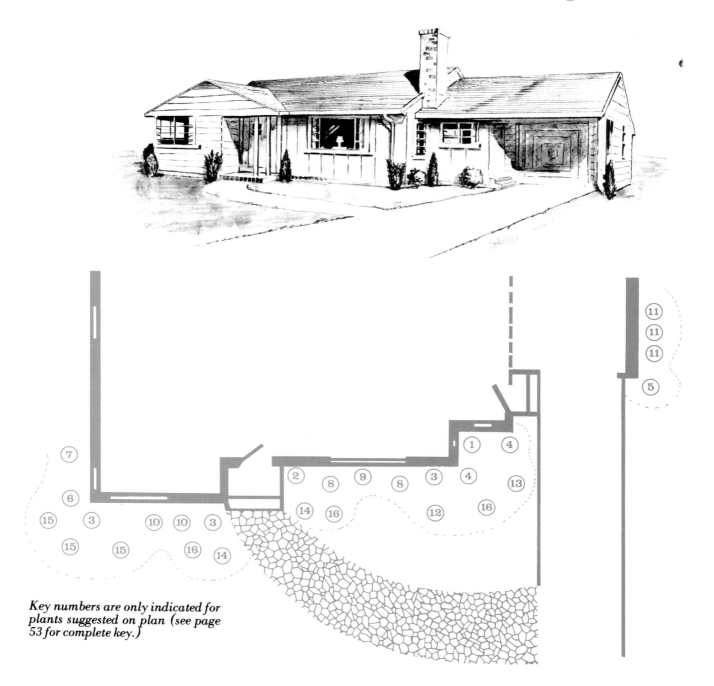

Key numbers are only indicated for plants suggested on plan (see page 53 for complete key.)

EVERGREENS as corner plants

Variety	Special features	Location
Pyramidal Cedar (1)	Pyramidal shape, dark green foliage	Sun or partial shade
Cannarti Juniper (2)	Pyramidal shape, lustrous green foliage	Full sun, light soil
Silver Juniper	Pyramidal shape, silver blue foliage	Full sun, light soil
Hick's yew (3)	Columnar shape, dark green	Sun or shade

FLOWERING SHRUBS as corner plants

Variety	Special features	Month of Bloom	Location
Double Orange Blossom (7)	Large white flower	June	Sun or partial shade
Bridal wreath	White flower	July	Sun or partial shade
Forsythia (in variety)	Yellow flowers before leaves appear	April & May	Sun or partial shade
Hydrangea P.G. (6)	White to pink cone-shaped flowers	August to November	Sun or partial shade
Beauty Bush	Graceful shrub with pink bell-shaped flowers	June & July	Full sun
Golden mock Orange (4)	Yellow leaves, white flower	June	Full sun

Climbing vines on a trellis (or self clinging) may be effectively used as "Corner Plants"

Variety	Special features	Month of Bloom	Location
Clematis Jackmanii (5)	Large purple flower	July & August	Full sun
Silver lace vine	Lacy white flowers	July & August	Full sun
Goldflame honeysuckle	Bi-color yellow and red flower	June to November	Full sun

EVERGREENS as entrance plants

Variety	Special features	Location
Hick's yew (3)	Dark green, withstands most abuse	Sun or shade
Blaauw's blue juniper	Fine foliage, very hardy	Full sun
Cannarti juniper (2)	Lustrous green foliage	Full sun, light soil
Silver juniper	Silver blue foliage	Full sun
Pyramidal cedar (1)	Dark green foliage	Sun or partial shade
Mugho pine	Use on either side of low steps	Sun or partial shade

FLOWERING SHRUBS as entrance plants

Variety	Special features	Month of Bloom	Location
Double mock orange	Large white flower	June	Sun or partial shade
Golden mock orange (4)	White flower Yellow leaves	June	Full sun, trims well, may be used with low steps
Weigelia (in variety)	Red or pink flower	July & August	Sun or partial shade
Silver leaf dogwood	Variegated leaves	Used for foliage color	Partial shade or sun
Snowberry	Small rose colored flower White berries	June & July October to December	Shade or sun
Flowering quince	Red or pink flower	April & May	Partial shade or sun

NOTE: The above lists are only **suggestions**. There are many others which could be used just as effectively.

STEP 2 ~ Under the window plantings

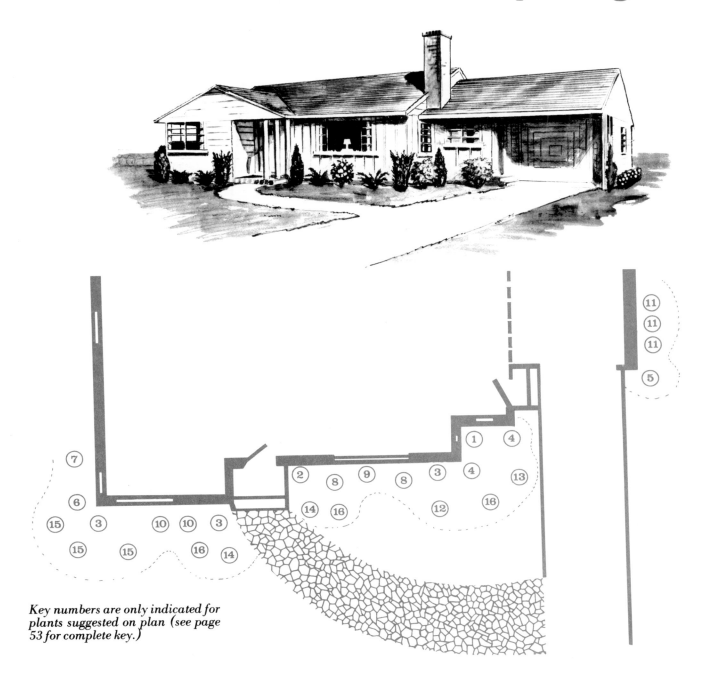

Key numbers are only indicated for plants suggested on plan (see page 53 for complete key.)

EVERGREENS as under the window plants

Variety	Special features	Location
Blaauw's blue juniper	Fine foliage, semi-upright	Full sun
Blue Danube juniper	Blue green, vase-shaped	Full sun
Pfitzer juniper (8)	Medium green, spreading	Sun or partial shade
Meyer's juniper	Blue foliage, semi-upright	Full sun
Savin juniper (10)	Spreading, vase-shaped	Sun or partial shade
Golden pfitzer juniper	Golden foliage, flat spreading	Full sun
Silver King juniper	Silver blue, spreading	Full sun

Pfitzer's juniper has a 4 to 5 foot spread

Gold tipped juniper

Shearing spoils the natural beauty of any evergreen or shrub

FLOWERING SHRUBS
as under the window plants

Variety	Special features	Month of Bloom	Location
Red leaf barberry	Maroon red leaves all season	Use for colorful foliage	Full sun
Golden mock Orange	Golden leaves White flowers	June	Full sun. Trims well for "Under the Window" use
Hydrangea Hills of Snow (11)	White flowers	July & August	Sun or shade
Weigelia Bristol Ruby	Red flowers	July & August	Sun or partial shade
Grandiflora roses (9)	Various colors as listed	June to November	Full sun
Floribunda roses	Various colors as listed	June to November	Full sun
Dwarf Alpine currant	Dark green leaf, trims well, yellow flower	May & June	Shade or sun

*The plants selected will vary with the height that the windows are above the ground level. These are only suggestions. Other varieties may be used depending on the climatic conditions (hardiness), color required, and availability.

STEP 3~Facer plants, ground covers & bank binders

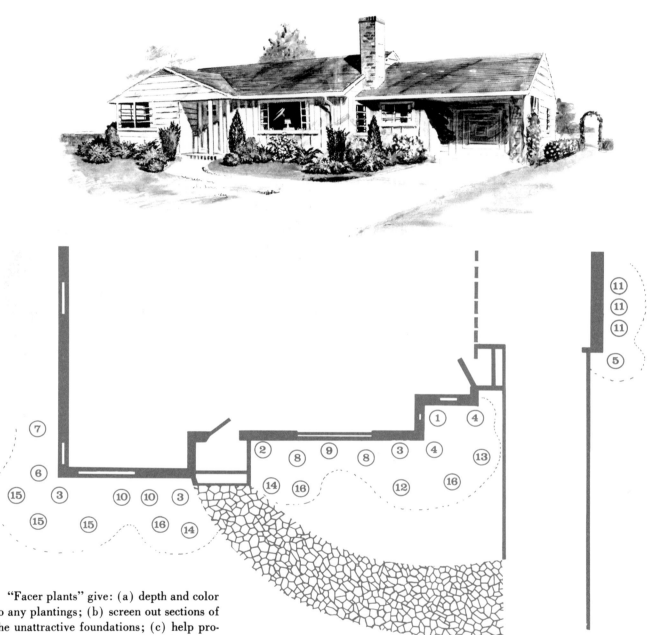

"Facer plants" give: (a) depth and color to any plantings; (b) screen out sections of the unattractive foundations; (c) help protect evergreens at entrances and corners from damage by dogs and children (e.g. barberry in semi-circle fashion in front of a silver juniper).

With tall houses, plantings on the corners should be "stepped". Use tall shrubs next to the house (2 ft. out from foundation). Then medium growing ones, and finally the smaller or lower growing shrubs. This "stepping" in size tends to make the house appear lower and wider, thus blending in better with the surrounding landscape.

Key numbers are only indicated for plants suggested on plan (see page 53 for complete key.)

FOR ADDITIONAL SPRING, SUMMER AND FALL COLOR

Spring bulbs (April and May); geraniums (June to September); and Cushion mums (August to November) are very effective planted among evergreens and shrubs in the foundation planting. A wide choice of individual varieties of striking color permits the establishment of an all-season color presentation.

49

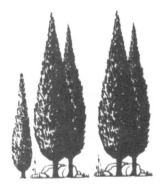

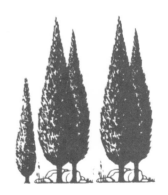

EVERGREENS as facer plants

Variety	Special features	Location
Dwarf Mugho pine (14)	Global, medium green-candle-like growth	Sun or partial shade
Dwarf Japanese yew	Spreading, dark green foliage	Full shade or sun
Globe cedar	Global, light green foliage	Sun or partial shade
Silver King juniper (13)	Spreading, silver blue foliage	Full sun
Tamarix juniper (12)	Spreading, bluish-green feathery foliage	Full sun

FLOWERING SHRUBS as facer plants

Variety	Special features	Month of Bloom	Location
Red leaf barberry (16)	Maroon red leaves	Colored foliage	Full sun
Green barberry	Crimson colored Fall foliage	Red berries	Sun or partial shade
Red spiraea	Red flower	June & July	Sun or partial shade
Blue Mist spiraea	Blue flowers in Fall	August to November	Full sun, light soil
Floribunda roses	Various colors as listed	June to November	Full sun

GROUND COVERS & BANK BINDERS

"Ground covers" are used among shrubs in foundation plantings; or as edgings; under large trees; along walks or in small areas (narrow space between walk and foundation of the house). Very colorful and practical on terraces when used as bank binders to prevent soil erosion.

Variety	Special features	Planting distance apart
Periwinkle (Vinca)	Green glossy foliage Blue flower—good in shade, excellent in full shade	6 in. to 9 in.
Japanese spurge	White flower	6 in. to 12 in.
Euonymus vegetus	Evergreen foliage, does well in shade	12 in.
Engelman's Ivy	Fall color, self-clinging	3 feet
Sub-zero Thorndale hardy ivy	Keeps leaves all year Will grow in full shade	2 feet
Goldflame honeysuckle	Fragrant bloom, partial shade or sun	3 ft. to 4 ft.
Silver lace vine	White flower, fast growing, plant in full sun	3 ft. to 5 ft.

The completed landscape plan

Having completed the "foundation planting" immediately in front of the house, consideration should be given to the planting on the remaining parts of the property. Select flowering shrubs to give a continuity of bloom and color during the Summer months. Hydrangea (both "Pee Gee" and "Hills of Snow") with their large cone-shaped and snowball flowers are very effective as a low screen along the side of a bare wall (e.g. along the side of a garage).

Floribunda roses or Blue Arctic willow makes a colorful border or edging for a patio. To complete the planting in the "front area", a decision should be made as to whether a hedge is desired across the front as well as along the sides of the lawn — or just at the sides (outlining property boundaries). A hedge across the front gives privacy; cuts down dust and road noise. However by leaving the front open to the street you can make a small lot appear much larger.

Give serious thought to the location of plantings which will create special interest such as rose beds, perennial borders, and specimen trees and shrubs to complete the "front lawn" planting.

THE "OUTDOOR LIVING ROOM"

This is the area which lends itself to developing something different and original with personal innovations which will make it unique.

Barbecues; sun dials; picnic tables; pools; rockeries; patios; etc., should be located now on your plan (even if not constructed immediately). Place the trees and shrubs to give maximum privacy; desired shade, and a pleasing pictorial effect.

Maintain "balance" by establishing a focal point (e.g. a bench, arbor or specimen tree). Place this focal point opposite the section of your home from which the scene will be most often viewed — generally from the patio or living room window. Develop both sides of the line of axis of the focal point proportionately. It is better not to dot the lawn area with trees and shrubs. Leave the centre lawn area clear. Shrubs and trees should frame the picture.

In informal gardens, avoid straight lines. Flower and shrub beds with curved outlines give a soft pleasing effect.

Automatic watering makes watering the lawn easier

Create areas of special interest around your home

51

A well kept rockery will add considerable interest and is fascinating and attractive.

Do not place plants too close together. Keep in mind the ultimate height and spread; otherwise they will grow together and lose their individuality and spoil the overall final effect. If the planting appears too thin the first year or so, supplement it with perennials or roses which may be moved to another location at a later date.

THE "SERVICE AREA"

Locate the "service area" where it is readily accessible and easily seen from the kitchen window, especially if it is being used for a drying yard or as a children's play area. Having determined the location and size, then decide what kind of hedge will be used to separate it from the "outdoor living room" area. If using a fence, add color by planting climbing and rambling rosebushes.

FRUIT AND VEGETABLE GARDEN

Always include dwarf fruit trees (even in your perennial or shrub border), if you do not have room for a separate fruit garden. Not only do they bear delicious large sized fruit, but are very colorful both for bloom and fruit. Strawberries, raspberries, currants and gooseberries picked from your own garden taste so much better and require little space. Grape vines are very desirable over a trellis or on a dividing fence.

Ground plan for completed project

52

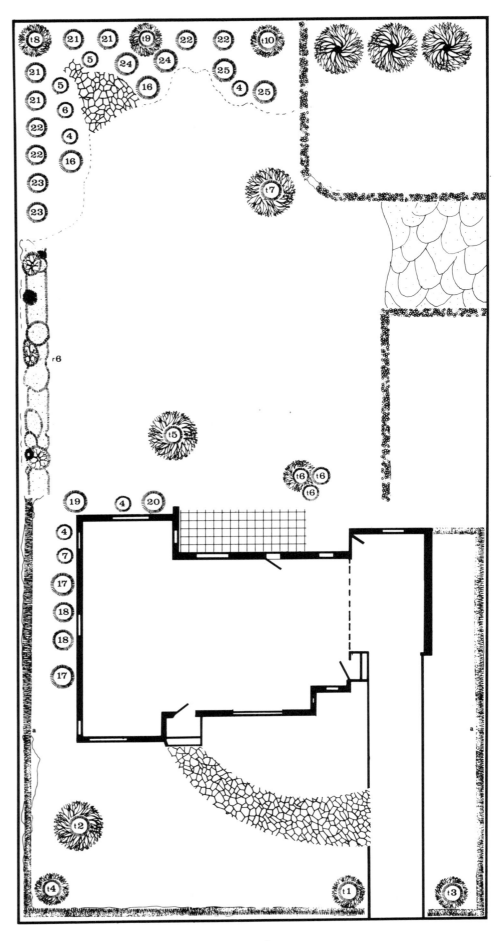

Key for materials

TREES

Key	Variety	Special features	Month of Bloom
T1	Koster blue spruce	Metallic blue needles	Blue all year
T2	Flowering crab (Van Esselstine)	Dark pink double flowers	May
T	Magnolia	Tulip-like pink flowers	April
T4	Red Japanese Maple	Blood red leaves all Summer	April
T5	Crimson King Maple	Maroon red leaves	Planted for colored foliage
T6	Clump silver birch	White bark, green leaves	Planted for white bark
T7	Flowering thorn	Bright red flowers	May & June
T8	Catalpa Speciosa	Huge white flowers	June
T9	Purple leaf Plum	Pink flowers, planted mainly for colored foliage	May
T10	Flowering crab (Almey)	Fiery crimson red flowers	May
1.	Pyramidal cedar	Pyramidal, dark green	Green all year
2.	Juniper cannarti	Pyramidal, light green	Green all year
3.	Hick's yew	Columnar, dark green	Green all year
4.	Golden mock Orange	Yellow leaves, white flower	June
5.	Clematis Jackmanii (vine)	Large velvet-like purple bloom	June to September
6.	Hydrangea P.G.	White to pink cone-shaped flower	August to November
7.	Double Orange blossom	White fragrant flower	June
8.	Pfitzer juniper	Flat spreading	Green all year
9.	Grandiflora roses	Long flowering	June to October
10.	Savin juniper	Vase-shaped, spreading	Green all year
11.	Hydrangea Aborescens	Large snowball flower	July & August
12.	Tamarix juniper	Low, flat, spreading	Green all year
13.	Silver King juniper	Silver, low, flat, spreading	Green all year
14.	Mugho pine	Global, candle-like growth	Green all year
15.	Green barberry (trimmed)	Scarlet foliage in Fall	Red berries in winter
16.	Red barberry (trimmed)	Maroon red leaves	Planted for colored foliage
17.	Forsythia (Lynwood Gold)	Yellow flowers before leaves appear	April
18.	Weigelia Rosea	Pink bell-shaped flowers	July & August
19.	Beauty bush	Pink flowers, very floriferous	July & August
20.	Lilac (French hybrid)	Very fragrant, color varies with variety chosen	June
21.	Honeysuckle (Zabeli)	Very fragrant, red flower, red berries in Fall	June
22.	Lilac (Persian)	Mauve flower	July
23.	Weigelia (Bristol Ruby)	Red bell-shaped flower	July & August
24.	Flowering quince	Pink or red flower before leaves appear	April & May
25.	Flowering almond	Pink flower before leaves appear	May

HEDGING

Key	Variety	Special features	Month of Bloom
A	Amur river privet (Ligustrum amurense)	Trims readily Small white flower, very hardy	June
B	Alpine currant (Ribes alpinum)	Dark green, small yellow flower	June
C	Double mock orange	White flowering	June

PERENNIALS

P—Perennial border—Color is a perennial border's greatest gift. Select tall growing varieties for near positions and choose kinds that permit a variation of color from early Spring to snowfall.

ROSE BUSHES

Key	Variety	Special features	Month of Bloom
R1	Hybrid tea, floribunda, or grandiflora roses	Everblooming In variety of colors	June to November
R2	Floribunda rose hedge	Continuous flower	June to November
R3	Hybrid tea rosebed	Continuous flower	June to November
R4	Grandiflora roses	Tall growing, everblooming	June to November
R5	Climbing roses	A mass of color	June to October
R6	Rugosa rose hedge	Extremely hardy	July to September
R7	Climbing or rambler roses on fence	Long flowering	June to October

Tree roses help to beautify any garden

This charming dwarf floribunda rose grows only 12 inches high

54

PLANS ACCORDING TO STYLE

PLANS ACCORDING TO STYLE

A limited budget planting

This plan consists entirely of deciduous (not evergreen) plants. By so doing we obtain maximum results for a minimum expenditure.

The unlandscaped home shown here has three problems which must be considered when planning the landscaping.

1. A high unattractive foundation which should be screened.

2. Very little space between the foundation and the sidewalk.

3. Little distance between the driveway and the lot line.

In addition to the high foundation, the windows on the right side of the home are also comparatively high. This permits the use of larger deciduous shrubs with lower growing ones planted in front and in between. These shrubs not only screen the

foundation but also make the house appear wider and lower.

A low trimmed hedge (or drought resistant perennials) is suggested in the small space between the sidewalk and the foundation, under the living-room window. e.g. Blue Arctic willow, Dwarf Alpine currant or Stonecrop (Sedum spectabilis). Concrete foundations, especially with heated basements, tend to dry out the soil. Only varieties requiring little moisture will succeed in such locations.

Since there is not room for a large shrub or small tree on the left side of the driveway, we have suggested a barberry hedge ("B") planted "L" shaped at the driveway entrance. Inside the "L" area a specimen shrub could be used (No. 12 on plan), such as smoke bush, burning bush, purple leaf plum or tamarix.

A semi-informal flowering hedge ("C") completes the framing of the front lawn area.

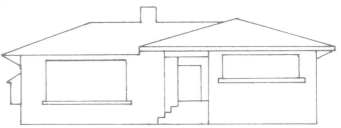

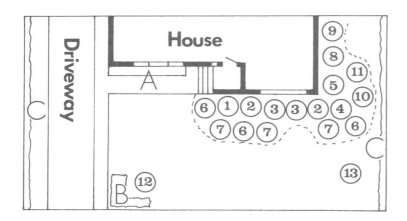

Key	Variety	Special features	Month of bloom
1.	Golden mock orange (Philadedphus aureus)	Yellow leaves, white flower	June
2.	Flowering plum (Prunus triloba)	Double pink flowers before leaves appear	May & June
3.	Beauty bush (Kolkwitzia amabilis)	Pink flowers, very floriferous	July & August
4.	Flowering quince (Cydonia)	Pink or red flowers before leaves appear	April & May
5.	Pee Gee Hydrangea	White changing to pink cone-shaped flowers	August to November
6.	Red Barberry (Barberis thun. atro.)	Maroon-red leaves all season	Used for foliage color
7.	Dwarf Alpine currant (Ribes alpinum)	Small yellow flower, attractively shaped leaf	Used for foliage color
8.	Golden spiraea (Golden ninebark)	Yellow leaf, white flower, brownish fruit in Fall	June
9.	Butterfly bush (Buddleia) (in variety)	Long flower spikes, (red, white, pink, mauve)	July & August
10.	Hills of Snow hydrangea (Hydrangea arborescens)	White snowball flower	July & August
11.	Weigelia Bristol Ruby	Red bell-shaped flower	July & August
12.	Smoke bush (Purple leaf (Rhus cotinus atrop)	Purple foliage and pink flower	July
13.	Mountain ash (Sorbus aucuparia)	White flower, orange berries in Fall	June

(A) Arctic Blue willow or Alpine Currant hedge
(B) Green barberry or Red barberry hedge
(C) Double white mock orange or Bridal Wreath spiraea hedge

Obtain maximum results for a minimum expenditure

Split level contemporary styled home

To "dress up" this home with shrubs and trees, consider the following:

1. A high wall and foundation on the right side of the house.

2. Lack of balance caused by the long sloping roof over the garage.

3. The entrance to the home (breeze-way) should be made more inviting.

The very high foundation at the right side of the house could be screened by using tall deciduous shrubs, properly faced by medium and low growing shrubs.

To make this part of the house more interesting, we have suggested placing a low retaining wall out from the house eight to ten feet. Note—the terraced wall need not necessarily be at right angles to itself or the house — but creates more interest if constructed on an angle as shown in plot plan. On this newly made terrace we then use a combination of evergreens, shrubs, roses and vines to establish a very attractive planting. The house now has a "new look".

A clump birch to the left and in front of the home, and a larger tree such as moraine locust or Norway maple to the rear of the house (which will grow higher than the garage), gives the picture the complete balance which we set out to do.

Make the entrance more inviting by planting a trimmed hedge on either side. This entrance planting is carried under the windows of the living room with a small group of "corner" and "spacer" evergreens planted in front in the semi-circle of the hedge.

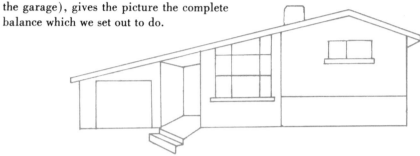

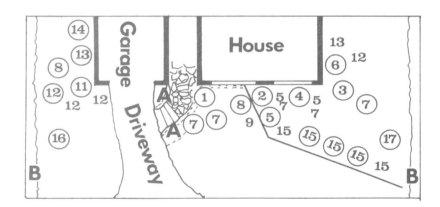

Plantings for this plan

Key	Variety	Special features	Month of bloom
1.	Cannarti juniper	Pyramidal, light green	Green all year
2.	Silver juniper	Pyramidal, silver-blue	Silver-blue all year
3.	Hick's yew	Columnar, dark green	Green all year
4.	Grandiflora rose	Long blooming	June to November
5.	Red barberry (trimmed)	Maroon-red all year	Used for colored foliage
6.	Pyramidal cedar	Pyramidal, dark green	Green all year
7.	Tamarix juniper	Low spreading	Blue-green all year
8.	Golden orange blossom (trimmed)	Yellow foliage, white flowers	June
9.	Savin juniper	Vase-shaped, spreading	Green all year
10.	Silver king juniper	Low spreading, silver foliage	Silver all year
11.	Hick's yew (trimmed)	Dark green, new growth lighter	Green all year
12.	Green barberry	Crimson foliage in Fall	Red berries in late Fall
13.	Flowering plum	Double pink bloom	May & June
14.	Forsythia	Yellow flower before leaves	April
15.	Sub-zero thorndale ivy	Glossy green leaves	Green all winter
16.	Clump silver birch	White bark, yellow foliage in Fall	Used for white bark
17.	Flowering thorn	Bright red flowers	May & June
A.	Alpine currant hedge (trimmed)	Trims well, dark green leaf	May & June
B.	Amur River privet hedge (trimmed)	Very hardy, most popular variety	June

Fluorescent lighting makes indoor gardens more feasible

The ranch type house

The modern low ranch type home seems to be the least difficult to landscape; yet provides an opportunity for considerable variation.

We should, however, watch the following points:

1. Careful selection of plant materials which ultimately will not grow too large for this low type of structure, and eventually grow out of bounds.

2. Since we have attractive and expensive masonry, it should be complimented with plants rather than screened.

3. Large shade and ornamental trees should not be planted near the home.

To recommend a plan which is different, we have left a considerable lot of open area for additional "color planting". We suggest that the area bounded by the driveway, the sidewalk and the front porch be made the point of interest. Use as a basic plant an Upright evergreen in the center, surrounded by four flat spreading evergreens to give all season color. This area is framed with a low trimmed formal hedge. With this type of bed additional summer color can be varied from year to year by using such colorful plants as Spring flowering bulbs, floribunda, miniature and hybrid tea rosebushes, geraniums, begonias and finally for a riot of Fall blooms, chrysanthemums.

On the balance of the plan we have suggested low growing and spreading evergreens spaced far enough apart to allow the attractive masonry to appear between the plants. If additional color is required during the Spring, Summer and Fall months, tulips, floribunda roses, dwarf Cushion chrysanthemums and various varieties of low growing perennials, may be planted among these evergreens. Keep evergreens well out from the foundation to afford an ample supply of moisture for feeder roots at all times.

Koster blue spruce with its brilliant glistening silvery-blue color is the first choice as a specimen tree on the right hand side. This outstanding variety is attractive twelve

months of the year especially decorated with lights during the Holiday season.

On the left side a flowering crab will be ideal. Other specimen trees for this location would be flowering thorn, purple leaf plum or mountain ash.

An Amur River privet hedge across the front of the property is optional but will cut down dust and road noise, besides giving additional privacy.

Although we have shown a planting which is predominantly evergreen, deciduous shrubs could be used in a similar manner, providing the lower growing varieties were selected. Do not make the planting too crowded with either evergreens or shrubs.

Additional summer color can be varied from year to year

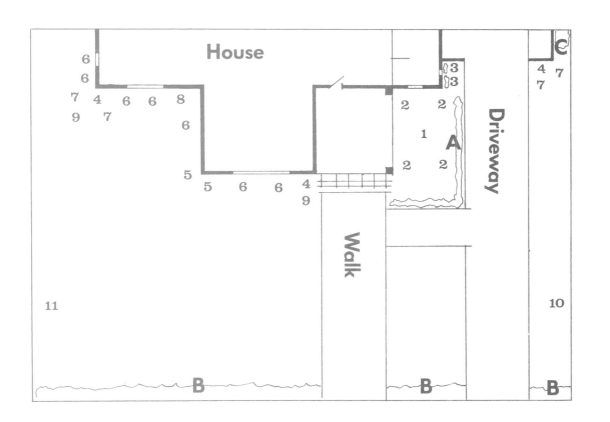

House

6
6
7   4   6   6   8
9   7
6

5
5   6   6   4
9

C
3
3
4
7

2   2
1   A
2   2

Driveway

Walk

11

10

B   B   B

Plantings for this plan

Key	Variety	Special features	Color of foliage
1.	Alberta spruce	Very dwarf, slow-growing	Light green
2.	Silver king juniper	Low spreading	Silver-blue
3.	Euonymus Vegetus	Broadleaf evergreen	Dark green, new growth light green
4.	Hick's yew (trimmed)	Trims readily	Dark green
5.	Hick's yew	Naturally columnar	Dark green
6.	Blue Danube juniper	Vase-shaped, spreading	Blue-green
7.	Pfitzer juniper	Flat spreading	Light green
8.	Cannarti juniper	Pyramidal shape	Light green
9.	Mugho pine	Global, candle-like growth	Medium green
10.	Koster blue spruce	Best evergreen lawn specimen	Silvery-blue
11.	Almey flowering crab	Crimson bloom in Spring, red fruit in Fall	Used mainly for Spring bloom

Low dwarf hedge

Key	Variety	Special features	Color of foliage
A.	Korean Boxwood	Broadleaf evergreen, slow growing	Light green
	or		
	Blue leaf Arctic willow	Trims well, very fine branches	Blue-green
B.	Amur River privet	Very hardy	Dark green
C.	Alpine Currant	Very compact	Dark green

A rock wall and steps do much for the appearance of this ranch style house

The story & one half & two story home

This type of home is usually quite high in proportion to the width. We have the following problems.

1. To screen the high foundation which is showing above ground level.

2. Te endeavour to make the house appear wider and lower. We have two choices

(a) construct a full terrace as shown. either of grass, stone or concrete,

(b) use various heights of shrubs to reduce the apparent height of the house.

Using a full terrace as shown here, it not only appears to lower the house, but provides a more attractive entrance, with only one step at the front door instead of several.

Having constructed the terrace (grass or stone), use deciduous shrubs faced with spreading evergreens, which gives a lower, flatter appearance. Carry the shrubs well outside of the corners of the house, making it appear wider and lower. On the plan and in the picture we have shown a grassed terrace at the front and side of the house. However, if you prefer a type of terraced dry wall, it can be easily constructed with laid in stone, or you may even desire a solid concrete type of terrace wall.

As an alternative to the grass slope or dry wall in front of the terrace — flat colored stones could be used very effectively. The stone follows the contour of the slope and is not a wall, but is simply stones of different shapes placed on the soil instead of grass. Additional interest and color may be obtained by using low growing, drought resistant plants (e.g. Sedum acre) planted between the stones.

If you do not feel that you wish to build the terrace, then another solution to the problem is to use large flowering shrubs faced with medium and low growing shrubs, which reduces the height of the house and hides the foundation wall. In addition a medium to tall growing hedge across the front of the property would further reduce the apparent height, without the use of a retaining wall.

To lessen our consciousness of the height of the house, create an additional point of interest by adding a perennial border in front of a flowering informal hedge at the extreme left of the lot. Complete the picture by placing a large specimen shrub at the end of the perennial border, (between the hedge and the house). Large growing trees in the background will add considerably to the overall picture.

The original height of the home is no longer noticed, as the house seems to nestle and become part of a colorful and interesting picture.

Chrysanthemums brighten the foundation bed

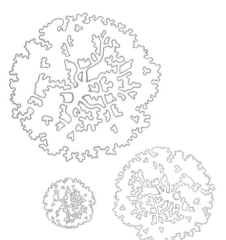

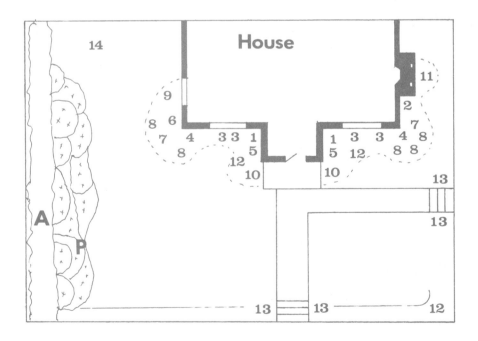

Story & one half

Key	Variety	Special features	Month of bloom
1.	Pyramidal cedar	Pyramidal	Green all year
2.	Double flowering mock orange	White flowers	June
3.	Golden mock orange	Golden leaf, white flower	June
4.	Fragrant viburnum	Fragrant, white bloom	May & June
5.	Hydrangea Arborescens	White snowball flower	July
6.	Flowering quince	Pink and red flower, varies with variety	May
7.	Prairie almond	Pink flower	May
8.	Green barberry	Colored foliage	Winter berries
9.	Weigelia rosea	Pink flowers	July
10.	Globe cedar	Global, dark green	Green all year
11.	Boston ivy	Self-clinging, fall color	Summer and Fall color
12.	Pfitzer juniper	Spreading evergreen	Green all year
13.	Savin juniper	Van-shaped, spreading evergreen	Green all year
14.	Purple leaf plum	Purple leaves	May & June
A.	Spiraea Van Houttie hedge (untrimmed)	White flowers	June

P. Perennial bed—Permits a wide selection of color, variation in height; and seasons of bloom; depending on personal choice of variety.

Large modern split level house

The modern split level house often has a combination of the problems already found in tall narrow homes (see one and one-half story; see page).

1. The tall two story section at the right requires a planting to reduce its height.

2. The one story section at the left often having a high foundation requires special screening.

3. The two plantings must be so combined to soften the lines of the house, thus making both sections appear as one in the overall picture.

4. We must blend the terraced lawn area into the driveway so that it appears as a gentle slope rather than an abrupt drop. Remember the lawn is sloping upwards from the street line to the house, and from the driveway upwards towards the walk which leads from the city streets to the front door.

Since the two story section has a very high front corner at the right of the garage entrance, it can be made to appear lower by planting large shrubs next to the building. As we progress out from the foundation step down the height again with medium and finally lower growing shrubs. A medium growing tree (mountain ash, silver birch or red chestnut) will further screen this corner, breaking the straight lines and diminishing the apparent height of this section of the building.

Dealing with the area immediately in front of the house, use a combination of deciduous shrubs and evergreens. Not only does this screen the foundation, but a tall specimen tree (e.g. crimson king maple, cut leaf weeping birch or Norway maple) planted on the lawn in front, and to the left of the one story section, will balance the picture.

To soften and enhance the terrace and the appearance of the steps in the terrace, plant a ground cover (e.g. vines, pachysandra or vinca minor), on the slope of the terrace ("A") from the street line to the steps. By continuing this ground cover in front of the shrub planting in the area between the garage and the front door, we have camouflaged the steps and blended together the entire planting of the two sections of the home into a balanced picture.

Climbing hydrangea

The Philadelphus or Mock Orange

Clematis

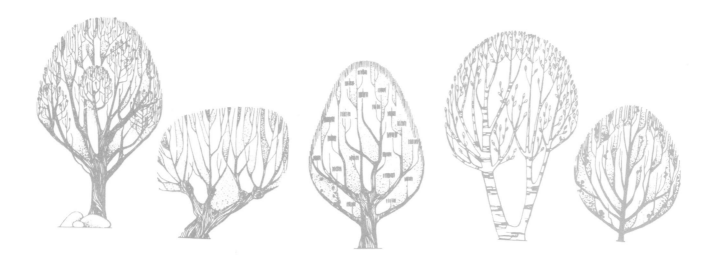

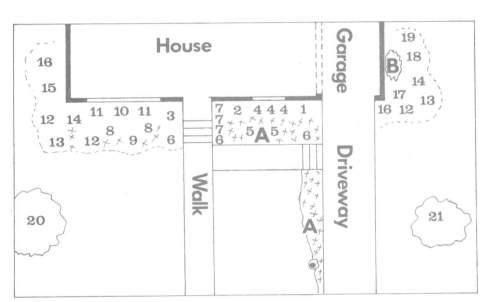

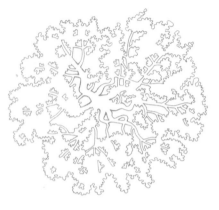

Key to plantings

Key	Variety	Special features	Month of bloom
1.	Pyramidal cedar	Pyramidal, dark green foliage	Green all year
2.	Cannarti juniper	Pyramidal, light green foliage	Green all year
3.	Hick's yew (trimmed)	Columnar, dark green foliage	Green all year
4.	Golden mock orange	Yellow leaves, white flower	June
5.	Silver king juniper	Silver foliage, flat spreading	Silver-green all year
6.	Globe cedar	Global, dark green foliage	Green all year
7.	Alpine currant (trimmed)	Dark green, compact shrub	May & June
8.	Savin juniper	Vase-shaped, spreading	Green all year
9.	Mugho pine	Global, candle-like growth	Green all year
10.	Floribunda or grandiflora rose	Color varies with variety, blooms all season	June to November
11.	Euonymus vegetus	Broad leaf, evergreen bittersweet	Green all year Orange berries
12.	Green barberry (trimmed)	Crimson leaves in Fall, compact shrub	Red berries in Fall
13.	Red barberry (trimmed)	Maroon-red leaves	Used mainly for colored foliage
14.	Flowering almond	Double pink flower before leaves appear	April & May
15.	Weigelia Bristol Ruby	Red bell-shaped flowers	July & August
16.	Silver leaf dogwood	Silver and green leaf, red bark	Used mainly for foliage
17.	Prunus triloba	Double pink flower	April & May
18.	Forsythia	Yellow flowers before leaves appear	April & May
19.	Golden spiraea	Golden leaf, white flower	May & June
20.	Crimson king maple	Maroon-red leaves all season	Used for foliage color
21.	Mountain ash	White flowers, orange or red berries	For colorful berries

Ground Covers

Key	Variety	Special features	Month of bloom
A.	Sub zero thorndale ivy or Pachysandra	Hardy, evergreen vine White flowers	Green foliage June

Climbing vine on trellis

Key	Variety	Special features	Month of bloom
B.	Clematis Jackmanii	Purple flowers	July to September

SPECIALTY GARDENS

Luxury Gardening for Pennies

Not too many years ago, in our mind's eye we pictured a millionaire's home with a glassed-in conservatory along its south wall or with a shiny glass greenhouse to the rear surrounded by cold frames and gardens.

Because of this mental picture, a private greenhouse was always thought of as a luxury, something far beyond the means of a suburban home owner. As a result, special growing structures such as greenhouses, hotbeds and plant starters have been neglected. Most gardeners fail to realize that a practical greenhouse is no longer a luxury. By the use of polyethylene plastic film over a simple wooden framework, a good sized-structure can be put up for about the cost of a bicycle, while often a cold frame can be knocked together without any cost whatever, using a discarded storm sash and second hand lumber.

Such structures need not be elaborate to be extremely useful. The simplest form of hotbed can produce so many annuals and vegetable plants that a good sized suburban lot can be planted with a generous hand. Without such a structure, most home owners have to skimp and will buy only a dozen or two annual plants when they should be using them by the hundreds. Even more than the money saved, any true gardener will get a thrill out of growing his own plants and producing them so cheaply that he can afford to use them freely.

If space out of doors is so precious that even an area six by six feet cannot be spared for a cold frame or hotbed, much of the work of starting seedlings, rooting cuttings and forcing bulbs can be done under fluorescent light in one corner of a basement where daylight never penetrates.

A very wide variety of plants can be grown in the smallest greenhouse

Types of Growing Structures

Cold Frames: This is the simplest form of plant-forcing structure. While not as useful as a hotbed or greenhouse (where the use of artificial heat extends the season many months) it can stretch the gardener's pleasure by many weeks. In Spring it allows him to gain at least a month in starting plants and during Fall he can protect plants against early frosts, extending the season a month or two at that end.

The Many Uses of a Cold Frame —

(1) Seeds can be sown directly in the frame to be transplanted outdoors later. These are usually half-hardy or hardy annuals and vegetables that need less heat.

(2) Quick-maturing vegetables such as lettuce and radishes can be grown to full size right in the frame, weeks before they can be seeded out of doors.

(3) Pots of bulbs, buried in the frame in Fall, will form roots and be ready for forcing from Feb. 1st on.

(4) Vegetables such as endive, Chinese cabbage and root crops can be stored over Winter in a frame.

(5) Half-hardy perennials can be carried over Winter without loss.

(6) Pansies and English daisies, sown in early Fall, can be carried over Winter in the frame then planted out with tulips and irises in Spring.

(7) Seedlings started in a greenhouse or sunny window can be "hardened off" in a cold frame so they will be ready for transplanting out of doors when warmer weather comes.

(8) A cold frame allows greenhouse space to be used for starting plants, which can then be stored temporarily in a cold frame.

A Hotbed speeds Growth — Every cold frame operation can be performed equally as well in a hotbed, even with the heat cut off. With the heat on, less hardy annuals and vegetables can be started without fear that sharp frosts will kill them.

In rooting cuttings, soil that is warmer

Work can be done in the greenhouse in any weather

Once the weather turns cold, chrysanthemums can be moved indoors for additional bloom

72

than the air (a condition called "bottom heat") will speed up rooting. In Spring, hardwood cuttings can be planted in the hotbed, rooting them long before they can be set out of doors. This often saves a year's time in producing a mature shrub. Even in Summer, if August and September nights are cool, bottom heat will stimulate rooting of softwood and half-hardy cuttings.

A hotbed can be used earlier in Spring and later in Fall. In Spring, there is no need to wait until sun heat warms the soil, turning on the heat will do this in a matter of hours.

Most greenhouse work can be done in a hotbed, except at the sacrifice of convenience. It is hard to lift sash, brush away snow and otherwise work with a hotbed at times. The decision to erect a greenhouse or make a hotbed might well hinge on this question of convenience.

Advantages of a Greenhouse —

Since work in a greenhouse is done while standing it is much less of a strain on the gardener. Too, it can be entered at any time, even when snow or rain make the operation of a hotbed a chore. Certainly, any gardener past middle age should consider a greenhouse, even though it be no larger than a double hotbed, six by six feet.

One warning should be given, however, if a greenhouse is operated the year around, it can be a hard taskmaster, demanding your presence during the day and at night under some conditions. A careful check of owners of small greenhouses, none larger than 15' x 20', showed that they averaged about six hours work a week in them the year around. More time was spent during Spring months, when seedlings for outdoor planting were being grown. February to April can be time-consuming.

It is possible to eliminate much of the work by the installation of automatic ventilating equipment, automatic humidity control, automatic heat and similar devices. However, some of these are expensive: automatic ventilation may easily double the cost of a simple greenhouse.

One way to reduce the amount of work needed is by operating the house only during Spring months to grow annuals and vegetable plants for the garden. However, this does away with one of the real pleasures of greenhouse gardening — the thrill of being able to smell damp earth and blooming plants in Winter.

Fluorescent Lights — Growing and propagating units lighted only by fluorescent tubes are a compromise between a greenhouse and a frame. All the work can be done while standing, so they are as convenient as a greenhouse in this respect. For starting seeds and rooting cuttings they are excellent, particularly if a cold frame is available outside to harden off seedlings and cuttings before they are planted out of doors. Plant growth under lights is quite soft and tender, because of this plants produced in a fluorescent unit and set directly in the garden, rarely survive.

One advantage of the completely enclosed fluorescent unit is that when conditions are good, it can go for a week or more without any attendance. Even a travelling man can use one, watering and tending it over the week-end. Moisture condenses and is re-used rather than being lost.

Lights must be close to the seedlings or cuttings. Fluorescent light does not "project" well and is effective only within a short distance. From 6″ to 12″ above the plants is about right. Two 40 watt tubes, suspended at that height, will light an area of flats or pots about four feet long and 24″ wide. When growing seedlings, use daylight white tubes as they need blue light.

Over a number of years a greenhouse should pay for itself

Some gardeners may only want to operate a greenhouse during the Spring months

73

Cuttings require warm white or reddish light.

If an open unit is used, such as lights suspended over a table in the basement, try adding a 25 watt ordinary incandescent or Mazda bulb; this often improves growth under lights. In an enclosed unit, it adds too much heat.

Every effort should be made to keep the temperature in an enclosed unit, or the air of a basement and the open unit as close to 68° as possible.

Vermiculite (available from most seed stores and garden centers) is the ideal growing medium for fluorescent units. Soil is too likely to be contaminated with disease organisms to be safe. For starting cuttings a mixture of half sand and half peat moss can be used.

If a white mould forms under artificial light, wash everything with a chlorine bleach and start over again.

About the only mature plants that thrive under fluorescent lights are African violets, some foliage plants and shade loving plants that can stand low light intensity. As a result, practically all the flowering plants grown in this way are African violets, which seem to thrive even if the tubes are kept lit 24 hours a day. They must be kept on for at least 16 hours for all plants, including seedlings and cuttings.

Surprisingly, few tulips and hyacinths are forced under fluorescent lights, although in Holland this is done commercially. Most of the growth of these plants is made while they are stored in darkness at temperatures below 50 degrees. When the shoots are three to four inches tall, the pots are placed under lights and kept there, with the lights turned on for 16 hours and off for eight in every 24, until they begin to open. They can then be brought into the living room for display.

CONSTRUCTION OF COLD FRAMES AND HOTBEDS

Construction of cold frames and hotbeds is somewhat alike. The site on which they are built should be in full sun, since sun heat is used to help warm them. If an electric cable is used in addition to sun heat (in a hotbed) the soil should be excavated to a depth of 10″ and a layer of sand four inches deep spread on the bottom. The electric cable goes over this, a layer of hardware cloth of ¼″ mesh (16 holes to the square inch) is laid over the cable and another layer of sand, two inches deep over the wire. Then a four inch layer of composted potting soil (see description later) is placed over the sand. If, however, cuttings are to be rooted, then sand, vermiculite or a mixture of sand and peat is used instead of soil.

For a cold frame excavate to a depth of four inches and fill the hole with either potting soil, with sand, peat and sand or with vermiculite.

Any spot used for frames should be on well-drained soils: nothing is worse for tender seedlings and cuttings than water standing around them. However, do not build up a mound and set the frame on top of this: the exposed sides will waste heat. Too, the soil inside may dry out too rapidly.

Wood for Construction — If wood is purchased to build frames, two inch thick planks are best for sides and ends. This provides some insulation, even when damp. One inch lumber is not too desirable. If, however, second hand boards one inch thick can be had for nothing, they can be used by making the sides double, with a layer of plastic or tarpaper between. Such walls are even warmer than two inch lumber.

Because the wood is practically always wet, it must be of some durable grade. Swamp cypress, redwood and western red cedar are the most durable, in that order. However, such woods are far from cheap. Less durable wood, treated under pressure with a preservative, can be used. This is usually treated with pentachlorophenol or some zinc compound. Wood treated with creosote is deadly to plants and should never be used.

About the only home treatment that is safe is to use copper naphthanate, a form of copper that resembles a liquid soap. It can be brushed on the wood, then allowed to dry thoroughly before plants are exposed to it. Once dry, it is harmless to plants. Home treatment with pentachlorophenol is not successful as the material

Some of the new window greenhouses have many uses

74

keeps coming out of the wood and as it is a fairly good weed killer it is harmful to all plants. Commercially-treated penta lumber is free from this trouble.

The frame should face south with the sash sloping in that direction. The back should be between 12″ and 16″ high, depending on what use is to be made of the frame. It is easy to raise pots of low plants on stands or boxes; for this reason a deep frame is more useful than a shallow one. A lower wall will make the frame useless for storing taller flowers, such as forced tulips in pots or flats.

The size will be determined by the size of the sash available if it is a discarded storm window. The sash should cover the upper edges of the wood sides, otherwise rain and snow can work down into the wood.

Commercial hotbed sash is made in three sizes — Junior, Half and Full. Junior sash is 24″ x 48″. Half sash is 36″ x 36″ and full size is 36″ x 72″. This is glazed with regular window glass, usually B grade single strength. However, glass is fragile and otherwise unsatisfactory and is rapidly being displaced with more modern materials.

The introduction of flexible polyethylene sheets made lightweight sash practical. Today, the size of a frame is limited only by the ease of working from its sides. Most gardeners find that 36″ is about as far as they can conveniently reach.

A sash covered with plastic film simply must be fastened down securely. Even a light wind can lift them allowing cold air to blow into the frame when not wanted. In a sheltered spot, glass-covered sashes can sometimes be left unfastened, but a stiff wind can easily lift them. Most common form of fastening is a rope with heavy weights (concrete blocks are good) tied onto each end.

Newest and perhaps best covering is fiber glass. If the flat type (sold by some greenhouse supply firms) can be obtained, it can be substituted for glass in standard hotbed sashes. The large flat sheet, however, is too flexible to use without additional support when covering a wide frame.

The corrugated sheet of fiber glass has many advantages. Not only is it quite rigid, but its corrugations catch every stray beam of light. In early morning and late afternoon, a frame covered with this material will be much lighter inside than one glazed with glass. Because of the corrugations, how-

An indoor greenhouse equipped with fluorescent lights can be used to grow many plants

75

Having a window greenhouse will give you as much fun as a full-sized one, but without maintenance, labour and expense of the larger size.

ever, some special shaped wood or rubber must be used at the top and bottom of the sash. This should fit into the corrugations and form a tight seal.

Hotbed Mats — Science has improved hotbed mats enormously. Once these were heavy, soggy masses of straw woven together with string. Nowadays, fiber glass wall insulation blankets can be sewn or stapled between flexible sheet plastic at home. This weighs less than one tenth as much as straw, yet is many times more efficient in saving heat.

Mats are placed over the sash to hold heat in the frame after sunset to retain the sun's heat. In extreme weather, they are sometimes left on cold frames during the day for temporary protection. Except in very windy weather they can usually keep frost out of a frame.

To conserve heat, commercial growers usually pile earth around the wooden sides during freezing weather, pulling it away in Summer so the wood has a chance to dry out.

Ventilating Frames — One of the most difficult problems in frame operation is that of proper ventilation. With sash in place, even on a zero day temperatures

inside may go quite high. In warmer weather, tender plants may even be cooked. For this reason, most gardeners leave a crack of air on the upper side of the sash on sunny days. Different thicknesses of wooden blocks allow the size of this crack to be adjusted to permit the excess heat to escape but retaining enough to keep the plants growing well.

GREENHOUSES

We do not intend to discuss large greenhouses, as most beginners will do well to confine their efforts to one not larger than 12′ by 15′. Even a house half that size, a lean-to six feet wide and fifteen feet long, can give a great deal of pleasure to the winter gardener. Since commercial glass houses come ready-cut with comprehensive plans for erection, their construction need not be discussed here.

The most difficult problem for an amateur to solve in a home-built greenhouse is that of ventilation. It is one of getting rid of excess heat, particularly in winter on sunny days. If vents are placed too close to the plants, a blast of cold air can injure them or check growth. For this reason, vents in home-designed houses should be placed at the ridge or peak of the roof, where heat accumulates and where it can be vented quickly.

The vent panel or window is usually a long, narrow frame along the ridge which can be opened by a push rod. Commercial ventilating equipment is available, operated either by a chain or a geared wheel. This type of equipment is only necessary if the ridge is 12 to 15 feet above the floor, but for the smaller house, push rods with holes along them will allow the sash to be opened to just the right point.

Wood — Development of modern wood preservatives has made the question of durable wood less important than previously. Formerly, it was a waste of time to use anything other than swamp redwood or cypress. These had to be milled to special shapes which provided space for glazing putty, grooves to catch the drip from the roof and to other special shapes for other parts of the greenhouse structure. If a conventional glass greenhouse is to be built, only a commercial greenhouse manufacturer can supply them, as well as the special fastenings and nails needed.

However, the do-it-yourself builder probably should not build such a house. True, if attached to a residence, the glass conservatory, particularly one with curved glass eaves, is perhaps the most attractive unit that can be built.

Polyethylene Flexible Plastic —
The advantage of this film is that the structure supporting it can be almost any convenient shape, so long as the roof drains well and the sun can strike the film for several hours a day to provide light. Commercial houses are made with half-circle trusses, with A-trusses and even shed type roofs. Ventilation is supplied either with push rod-operated vents as already described, or with fans as described later under fiber glass houses.

Fiber Glass Houses — This is the newest and in many ways the best of all greenhouse construction. Fiber glass is made by reinforcing a rigid plastic sheet with fibers of glass. In corrugated form, it makes the most efficient greenhouse roof known. The corrugations capture every stray beam of light, distributing this light uniformly throughout the interior.

As a result, in early morning and late afternoon, a fiber glass greenhouse is amazingly light as compared with one glazed with panes of glass. This extra light means

Some form of automatic ventilation will be needed for year-round operation

The plastic filler will slowly wear away under the force of rain, sun and snow. When the glass fibers are exposed, they transmit less and less light as the filler disappears. Usually, about every five years the sheets should be recoated with a liquid form of the material used to hold the fibers together. Firms which supply the sheets can usually supply the liquid.

Because of the corrugated form of fiber sheets, special mouldings are needed to make them weather tight. These are made either of redwood sawed to form or of rubber to be laid on wooden members and nailed through both sheet and moulding.

Nails — All nails used in cold frames, hotbeds and greenhouses should be hot galvanized. Usually it is best to buy these from a regular greenhouse manufacturer: those sold in some hardware stores are electro-galvanized and do not have a thick enough layer of zinc to last under severe green house conditions. If redwood is used as lumber, it offers a further problem, since is contains a natural wood preservative which will eat away exposed steel or aluminum. Brass screws were formerly used to hold redwood, but really good hot-galvanized zinc nails will do the trick for less money.

For holding down fiber glass, either lead-covered nails or those with a neoprene rubber washer under the head are used. These must be driven carefully, drilling first with a drill slightly smaller than the nail. If driven carelessly, the panel may be weakened.

Ventilation—Venting fiber glass houses with conventional ventilators is difficult because the corrugated shape makes a tight joint at the roof difficult. Most houses built

superior growth during much of the year. In Summer, when regular glass houses must be shaded, the fiber glass roof provides its own shading because the glass fibers break up and scatter the light so that no burning takes place.

One advantage of this scattering effect is that the angle of the roof to the sun's need not be calculated carefully. When designing a conventional glass house, it is necessary to calculate the pitch of the roof to within half a degree to take advantage of every stray ray of light during dull Winter weather. For this reason, in a fiber glass house it is possible to use a roof frame which meets at the ridge at an angle of 90 degrees and forms a 45 degree angle at the eaves.

Every amateur carpenter will appreciate how much this simplifies construction.

Another advantage of fiber glass is its superior insulating qualities. Heat loss is lower in Winter and sun heat gain lower in Summer. It is also stronger than glass, as well as tougher. Hail will not break it. The extra strength of fiber glass makes it possible to run the glass panel right to the foundation so the space under the benches receives some direct daylight. Space always is at a premium in a home greenhouse and

the use of the area under the benches almost doubles its usefulness.

Fiber glass panels come in sheets of various sizes and weights. Widths to cover 24″ and 48″ rafter spacing are common. Lengths are usually eight, ten and twelve feet. If the clear type is used (it is actually slightly transparent and not as clear as window glass) thickness is not too important: the heavier grade will allow wider spacing of roof supports and may save money. Although colored sheets are available, only the so-called clear grade should be used, since it transmits the most light.

Fiber glass sheets have one disadvantage.

A greenhouse can provide a steady supply of salad material

In most home greenhouses only two benches are installed

with this material are ventilated with electric fans. The so-called attic fan used for house cooling is excellent for this purpose. A 30″ to 36″ fan is large enough to ventilate most home greenhouses. Mount to the side from which the prevailing wind comes. In the opposite side of the house, mount a self-closing shutter.

The shutter opens when pressure built up by the fan presses against it and opens the vanes. A thermostat can be used to turn on the fan when the house gets too hot and to turn it off after temperatures drop.

Benches — Most greenhouse benches are made of wood. The wood should be either one of the really durable grades or be treated with copper naphtanate. Moisture conditions are very severe and any less durable material may rot out in less than a year.

In most home greenhouses, only two benches are installed, one on either side of the center walk. To provide extra space for potting plants, a movable table that fits across the aisle can be used. If this has a couple of small bins fitted onto the bottom, it will provide space for labels, trowels, etc., leaving the upper surface free for work space.

HEATING GREENHOUSES AND HOTBEDS

Electric Heat — Electric hotbed cables have made the old manure hotbed obsolete.

A greenhouse can also be a year-round recreation room

Many flowers and vegetables are easily grown in a greenhouse

Certainly, nothing can be more convenient and easier to use. The new types of electric heaters, which have heating wires inbedded in glass panels should be used, since they are safe under greenhouse conditions. Care must always be used in plugging them in, however, since so often hands are wet when working in a greenhouse.

Lighting and Heating at the Same Time — Cold frames can often be converted into hotbeds by stringing electric bulbs from the rafter supporting the sash. Along the sides, light sockets can be mounted. They should be spaced about 24″ apart. The bulbs to use are the flood light type having silvered reflectors and of 100 watts. They should be connected to a thermostat which turns them off when the frame warms up. The big advantage in using lights is that frames are often dark and the added light stimulates growth.

Lights in the Greenhouse—The same idea can be used in a greenhouse to increase heat in a certain area so a warm-weather crop can be grown in a house which is otherwise kept at a lower temperature. For example, when tuberose begonias and gloxinias are pre-sprouted in a "sweat box", this unit can be heated by electric lamps to advantage, without raising the temperature in the rest of the greenhouse above its normal range.

Heat from the Home Heating Plant—Fortunately, a home and a greenhouse need heat as a rule at different times. Often on sunny days, a greenhouse may become so warm that it can help heat the residence to which it is attached. Opening a door into the house will allow some of this heat to be used without wasting it out of the vents. Often this use of surplus heat will offset the extra fuel needed to keep the greenhouse warm at other times.

Steam is not usually suitable for heating small greenhouses

78

Most greenhouses made of fiberglass are ventilated with electric fans

tropical foliage plants have high humidity needs.

In Fall and Spring, it is better to open the vents or start the ventilating fan than to water for increasing air moisture. Outside air is more humid, at least if the heating apparatus is working. In late Spring, Summer and early Fall, sprinkling the walks with a fine spray will usually result in enough humidity.

Summer Shade—A fiber glass or polyethylene film covering, whether on a hotbed cold frame or greenhouse, needs no shading: the glass fiber breaks up direct sunshine. Ordinary glass however, lets through too much light at times. About the time tall bearded irises begin to flower, the glass should be sprayed with a shading compound. To make a shading whitewash, mix three pounds of whiting, (buy it at a paint store) with enough water to work it into a smooth paste. Add eight ounces of linseed oil, stirring thoroughly. To this mixture, add three gallons of water.

This shading compound will gradually wear away and by Fall will all but disappear. Lath shades that roll down the glass roof can be purchased from greenhouse manufacturers, but they are quite expensive. Cheap bamboo slat porch screens from

Hot Air Heat—Certain oil space heaters, if vented to a chimney can be used for greenhouse heating. Those with a blower can be mounted in a separate room and heat blown through grills into the greenhouse. This type of heat calls for extra humidity to make up for the drying effect of hot air heat.

Humidity — Plants thrive in an atmosphere so close to saturation at times that most house paints fail in a few weeks when used on interior wood surfaces. When a house is used for mist propagation (jet nozzles keep a fog of water in the air at all times) humidity approaches 100%.

To provide enough moisture for good plant growth calls for attention to certain details. A common mistake made by beginners is flooring the entire greenhouse with cement. While the center walk probably should be paved, if possible use crushed stone or gravel for this instead of cement. Leave the soil under the benches uncovered. If heating pipes run under the benches, an easy way to add humidity is to spray them with water when sprinkling.

At the same time, too much moisture can be as harmful as too little. Much depends upon the type of plants being grown.

African violets can stand high humidity which would kill cactus, while most of the

Most beginners usually start with a greenhouse not larger than 12′ x 15′

Japan work just as well and cost only a fraction as much. They are good for about two years use.

On cloudy days, the movable type of shading should be rolled up, to give plants in the greenhouse advantage of all light possible.

GREENHOUSE OPERATION

A mistake often made by beginners is to buy a book on commercial flower forcing, only to discover that the florist grower has an entirely different purpose in mind than the amateur. He does not grow specimen plants for enjoyment — he grows crops of flowers. His job is to hit the demand for a certain flower, such as lilies at Easter and poinsettias at Christmas, exactly on the day the plants are needed. The home greenhouse owner is not interested in a house full of bloom on one day that is completely empty the next, only to start over again.

Soil — Perhaps the greatest single problem the commercial grower has is to find good soil for filling his benches. He goes to great lengths to prepare it. Often pasture land is purchased which is then fertilized and mowed for a year or two in order to produce a thick, healthy sod. This sod is then stripped from the field, piled upside down in piles, fertilizer is sprinkled between the layers of clods and the entire mass allowed to rot for a year.

It is then run through a special soil shredder which screens out all stones, woody roots and other trash, leaving only a pile of rich, mellow loam.

The home gardener has a similar problem, although the area of bench to be covered or the number of pots to be filled is far, far less. He can resort to the compost pile. On a hidden corner of his lot, a level spot is prepared for the pile. If the soil is gravelly or very sandy, a shallow pit is dug to help trap more moisture.

Over this, weeds, sawdust, dried leaves, garbage, peat moss, wood shavings, dead plants from the green house or almost any vegetable or animal waste that will decay is piled. The first layer should not be more than four inches deep. Over this sprinkle a good mixed fertilizer as though you are dusting powdered sugar on a doughnut. This fertilizer is to feed the bacteria that break down the organic matter. Over this keep piling alternate layers of soil and organic matter, each about four inches deep, to a height of two or three feet.

Leave the upper surface dish shaped to catch moisture. If rain does not fall, water the pile with a hose, but do not saturate it and drive out all air. Soil bacteria need air as much as they do moisture.

In about six weeks, turn the pile over and over, mixing the layers thoroughly. If this is done in Fall, the soil should be ready to use in Spring; if in Spring, use it the next Fall.

A screen made out of hardware cloth with four holes to the inch (half-inch mesh) fitted onto a wooden frame can be used to screen the compost for use. If the soil used was rather heavy, use about one part of vermiculite to three parts of sifted compost.

Fertilizers for Greenhouse Use — A well-rotted compost made as described will probably grow good seedlings without any added fertilizer, up to the time they are planted out in the garden. It can be used for potting tulips and other bulbs for forcing, also without added plant food.

When, however, plants such as carnations, chrysanthemums and many foliage plants remain in pots for two months or more, some additional feeding will be needed. For this purpose, the most satisfactory are some of the dry chemical plant foods that are added to water and applied in liquid form. In liquid form, there is little possibility of "burning" or otherwise injuring plants.

However, most manufacturer's directions recommend too frequent or too liberal feeding for use in the greenhouse. Under glass, light is naturally restricted so plants do not make as good use of fertilizers. For this reason, use these liquid fertilizers only about half as strong as recommended on the package, or only use half as often. The important thing is to be sure they are "complete", that is, they contain minor elements in addition to the familiar nitrogen, phosphorus and potash.

Temperatures — In catalogs and reference books, temperatures for growing certain crops are often given. For example, chrysanthemums are listed as a 60° crop. This refers to the night temperature to be maintained in the greenhouse, not the reading during the day. Daytime readings will often run 10° to 15° higher, particularly if the sun comes out. Most of the plants an amateur will want to grow will do well somewhere between 45° and 65°. This is, of course, a wide spread and not all plants will thrive. For this reason, dividing the greenhouse is good practice. This is sometimes done by installing more pipes in one end and less in the other, but this trick does not work in a small structure.

If electric hotbed cable is run under one bench, it can be used for crops which prefer more heat, even though the house itself may not go above 50 degrees. In other cases, houses can be divided physically with a cheesecloth or plastic partition, but this is a nuisance in a small house when trying to go from one part to the other. If this method

The experienced home gardener can grow orchids with success

is used, extra heat should be installed in the warm end.

However, do not use electric lights to supply this extra heat if you are trying to force chrysanthemums because they are short day plants. This means they will not flower except during short Winter days, so if given extra light, they keep on producing leaves but no blooms. The same is true of poinsettias. While an Easter lily will bloom on either a short or long day, the more light it gets, the longer it will stretch, an undesirable reaction when short, sturdy plants are required.

Propagating Frames — The propagating frame or "sweat box" as it is called in the trade, is a useful device which allows one crop to get more heat and humidity than is needed by the rest of the greenhouse. It is nothing more than a cold frame or hotbed built right over a portion of a greenhouse bench. If this is to be used for rooting hardwood cuttings or evergreen cuttings, it need not be in the sun, but can be tucked in any lightly shaded spot. This is filled with sand and the lid closed to retain heat and moisture.

EQUIPMENT

In addition to tools useful in working soil in the open garden, certain special types of equipment will be needed. Pots, for instance, are almost essential, since home greenhouse owners usually want to bring their flowering plants into the house for decoration or want to give them away to friends.

Old fashioned clay pots still have their day. They are durable unless broken and do not lose their shape when plants are grown in them for a long period of time. Professional florists are now substituting thin plastic pots for clay for two reasons. One, breakage in commercial growing is high and two, plastic pots weigh less, saving shipping costs.

Peat Fiber Pots — Perhaps the most convenient pot for the home greenhouse owner is the new type made out of a mixture of peat moss and wood fiber, formed under high pressure. Most manufacturers mix a little fertilizer with the pulp so that the pot will not pull plant foods out of the soil, as it might otherwise. Roots grow right through the pot, so it does not have to be removed before the plant is set in the garden or moved to a clay pot for producing

Frilled tuberous begonias can be easily made to bloom during the Winter

a larger specimen.

These pots come in sizes ranging from 1¾″ up to 4″: the most commonly used are 2½″ and 3″ sizes, which will grow anything from a petunia to a tomato. They will usually last long enough to allow seedlings

of this kind to reach a safe size for planting out, even if weather delays that operation a week or two.

Flats — This term is often confusing to those who are not too familiar with green-

81

house operation. It applies to low boxes, usually not more than 3″ deep used for many purposes. Filled with soil, they are used for starting seedlings which are either transplanted into peat-fiber pots for further growing-on, or are set directly in the garden. They should be of some durable wood, such as red cedar or cypress. Plastic and metal flats are also available. An amateur carpenter can easily make his own from any suitable lumber. Even old wooden crates can be used as a source of material, if the wood is treated with copper naphthanate as recommended under wood for greenhouses.

Greenhouse Wheelbarrow—Usually, greenhouse aisles are so narrow that a conventional wheelbarrow will not go through. A special wheelbarrow, made not more than 18″ wide and with straight sides will be a tremendous labor saving in wheeling soil and other supplies into the house and wheeling out finished plants.

WHAT TO GROW

Because pot plants are easier to handle, most of the flowers grown under glass by amateurs are grown in this way.

African Violet — A universal favorite. Its one weakness is that it cannot tolerate cold water on its leaves. Always have a tempering tank for warming water to be applied to African violets, gloxinias and other soft-leaved tropical plants. Single leaves cut off the plant can be stuck in sand, stem end down and will soon produce new plants at the base of the leaf. Night temperature 60°.

Azalea — Gift plants can be carried over from year to year and if properly handled will flower each year. Use half acid peat moss and half composted soil to pot them. Test for acidity: they will not thrive in an alkaline soil. Keep temperature 60° at night from November to flowering. After flowering, plant out in light, filtered shade under oak trees. Should go through a period when air temperature drops to below 50° but not down to freezing; this sets flower buds.

Begonias — So-called wax begonias are easiest: they will keep flowering all winter. Raise plants from seed in bulb pans filled with good composted soil. Scatter seed on top of soil: cover pot with glass after *gently*

watering. Keep at 68° until seedlings can be transplanted into 3″ to 4″ clay pots. Grow at 55° to 60°.

Tuberose begonias should be started in a sweat box and then potted individually in 4″ peat-fiber pots if to be used in the garden, in 5″ to 6″ pots if to be grown for house and porch decoration.

Rex Begonias — Grown only for their wonderfully-colored leaves. Propagate by cuttings. Prefer 65° temperature.

Browallia — Grow from seed: the best blue flower for winter blooming. 50° to 55°.

Geranium—Root readily from cuttings. Start right in peat-fiber pots by filling 4″ pots with composted soil mixed 50-50 with sand. Will need to be fed once they root.

Gloxinia—Grow like tuberose begonias, but use only as pot plants. Magnificent bloom. Temperature 55-60°.

Poinsettia — Make cuttings in June or July. Keep pinching tops to make plants stocky until September 1st. Need at least 60°. Avoid drafts. Do *not* turn on electric lights to work in greenhouse at night, or poinsettias will not flower.

Primroses — Primula malacoides (the baby primrose) is particularly dainty. Primula obconica is also an excellent greenhouse flower. Start from seeds: they are handled by specialists in greenhouse materials. Start at 60° but grow seedlings at 45 to 50°.

Bulbs in Pots —

Easiest of all plants to grow are those started from bulbs because the flower is already formed inside.

Tulips, narcissi and hyacinths are available from most seed houses and garden centers, but don't use **regular garden varieties unless recommended for forcing.**

Pot bulbs as soon as received (Sept. - Oct.-Nov.) and plunge them up to the rim in a cold frame outside. If necessary to keep the bulbs from freezing (they root best at 35° to 45° and stop growing when frozen) cover with soil and put on the sash. Later should be shaded with a mat to keep out the sun, which might force temperatures too high. When shoots are 3″ out of the pot, take them into a warmer, but darker room.

Ideal temperature is about 50°. When foliage is nearly full height, give them daylight or fluorescent light until flowers begin to open, then take to a warmer place. Flowers will keep better if not allowed to get over 60 to 65°.

Tender Bulbs — Paperwhite narcissi and French-Roman hyacinths, as well as the prepared hyacinths from Holland (they are usually listed for Christmas flowering) can be started right in the greenhouse bench but try to keep heat about 45 to 50° until they bloom.

Amaryllis — This sensational flower grows much better in the greenhouse than in the house. Grow at 50° until brought into the house.

Freesias — A pot of freesias in bloom will scent a whole house. Plant 10 to 12 bulbs in an 8″ bulb pan. Before bulbs start, stick wooden stakes around entire pot and form a cage with string. Freesias cannot support their own flowers. Plant corms in August and grow at 55°. They should flower about Christmastime.

Crocuses can be easily forced into bloom in the greenhouse from Christmas onwards

Water Lilies and Garden Pools

cost would be practically nothing if use is made of materials that might be found around any home. Such a pool would be perfect for those who rent their homes, and for those who have just built new homes because it provides one of the quickest methods of landscaping known. All it really requires, is the ambition to construct one, because it certainly does not require any mechanical ability.

These tub and barrel gardens fit beautifully into comparatively small areas, and into difficult corners of big ones.

To construct a barrel pool simply cut down to a height of 18″, any wooden cask previously used for beer, wine, olives and the like. Sink the container 16″ into the ground, leaving a 2″ lip above the top of the lawn to keep out surface water. Stones or sod then can be built around the raised lip to blend it into the landscape.

A wooden tub should be sunk in the same manner.

Whether the miniature garden is made of either tub or barrel, new wood should be avoided if possible, for it is poisonous to goldfish. New wood can be aged quickly by slaking a chunk of lime in the new receptacle, letting it set for a few days, stir-

Water lilies are universally admired whether growing in a garden pool or wild in a country pond or small lake. There is no addition which can be made to any garden that will create more beauty, attract more attention — or provide more enjoyment for all the family, than a pool for water lilies and goldfish.

Every garden has a possible site for a pool. In fact, in an undeveloped front or back lawn, such a pool will help give the landscape an established, finished appearance.

Even a flower garden which has been in existence for a long time has a place for a water-lily pool. The placid surface of the water becomes a mirror for its own and surrounding flowers.

MINIATURE POOLS

Miniature pools constructed of wooden tubs, cut down barrels, old bathtubs or any other sturdy containers that can be easily sunk in the ground, are an inexpensive and easy way of starting a water garden. This type of pool is most suitable for the small garden or the inexperienced gardener. The

Water lilies require no raking, hoeing or other garden chores

A BARREL OF FUN IN THE FLOWER GARDEN

Miniature pools can be constructed of wooden tubs, sawed-off barrels or old bathtubs

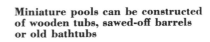

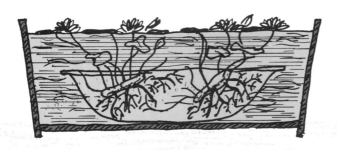

One or two lilies to each tub or barrel will be sufficient

Clusters of tub and barrel pools can be used in an unlimited number of patterns

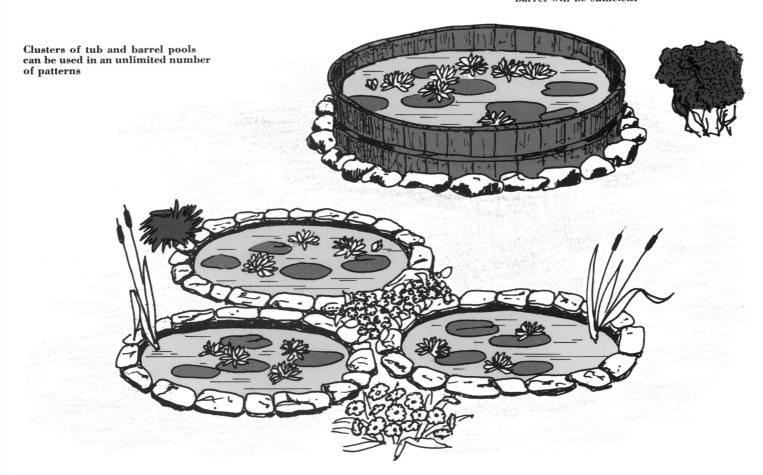

ring it occasionally, and then washing it thoroughly.

Water lilies can be planted in 4 inches of soil in the bottom of the barrel, or planted either in pots or other smaller receptacles, which then may be set in the bottom of the sunken container. A layer of sand spread on top of the planting soil will do much to improve the appearance of the pool.

Most beginners to pool gardening have a tendency to overplant. You will discover that one or two lilies to each tub or barrel will be plenty. There are several varieties of lilies especially adapted to culture in more or less confined spaces.

Building your own Water Garden —

With a professional cement craftsman doing the work, the construction of a back or side yard pool is a quick and comparatively inexpensive project.

With the owner doing the work himself, the project becomes an adventure in which the whole family can take part. This seems to be the trend at present, it gives the builder an added sense of creative achievement and is also less expensive.

After a site is chosen with an eye to its decorative value, other basic factors would be considered.

A garden pool adds beauty out of all proportions to its size

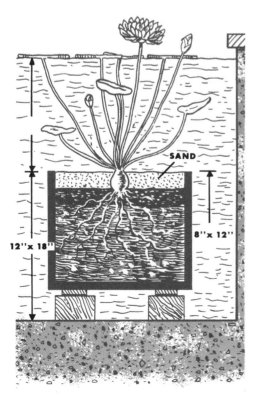

First, the pool should be situated so that, for a good part of the day at least, it is warmed by the sun. Water plants will not grow without sunlight.

If the excavation runs into clay, the builder can lay the concrete bottom directly upon the clay bed. Otherwise the bottom should be poured upon a 6-inch layer of well packed cinders. The bottom need not be more than 6 inches thick.

Shape and size of the pool are, of course, optional. A pool two feet deep is advisable for the culture of both water plants and goldfish. The walls, ideally, will be about 5 inches wide at the brim of the pool, thickening to 7-inches at the base.

One concrete mixture found highly satisfactory for pools is a combination of 1 part cement, 2 parts sharp sand, and 3 parts half-inch gravel or crushed stone, mixed to working consistency with water.

One underground pipe leading away from the pool can serve as both drain and over-flow pipe. The mouth of the drain in the bottom of the pool should be threaded so a 2-foot extension, the overflow pipe, can be attached. Normally, then, the pipe will carry away only the overflow. When the extension is detached at the mouth of the drain the whole pool can be emptied.

After the sides and bottom have set they should be smoothed over with a thin coat of cement applied with a trowel or paint brush. If the construction is then kept moist by frequent sprinklings over a period of 10 days, there will be practically no danger of alkali injuring the fish and plants when they are placed in the pool.

The new pool should be carefully washed out before it is stocked with water plants

BAG OF PLANT FOOD

Water lilies are family flowers

and fish. A vegetable growth, in the form of a green scum, may soon appear. It will disappear shortly, however, so do not change the water. And, above all, do not add chem-

In winter, set planting boxes on pool floor so root crowns will be safely below ice line

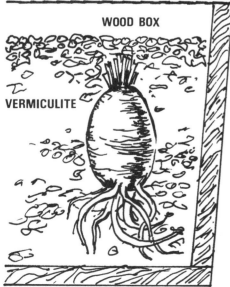

SCREEN

WOOD BOX

VERMICULITE

icals to the water, as they may injure the plants and fish.

WATER LILIES

The water lily is one of the world's most beautiful flowers. As a cultivated garden plant, it has few equals. By nature it is a vigorous, robust plant that demands only the bare essentials of sun, quiet water, and good soil in which to grow its best. It requires no raking, hoeing or any of the other gardening chores.

There are few flowers which have a longer blooming season. Water lilies will frequently bloom from some time in May until the first frosts in the Fall.

Water Lilies as Cut Flowers —

Water lilies floating individually in crystal bowls or arranged in a cluster to brighten a table or corner of a room, provide one of the most exciting and fragrant flower decorations a hostess can use.

You will discover that water lilies tie in beautifully with plans for any occasion. The day bloomers remain open during the early half of the day, with the night bloomers unfolding about 7 p.m., just in time for dinner. It is thrilling to see how they retain their fresh, natural beauty under artificial light.

The blooms can be kept open permanently if small drops of barely melted paraffin are applied by a medicine dropper to the lower extremities of stamens, petals and sepals. When using the wax it is advisable to tint it to match the color of the lily.

Planting and Winter Care of Water Lilies —

Water lilies are very rewarding. They start blooming with several flowers to each root, some time in May and continue until frost. They were considered expensive back in the days when they were grown principally on large estates in expensive surroundings. Today, they lie within the grasp of everyone.

Their main requirement is enough sunshine. These flowering aquatic plants need full sun all day if they are to grow and flower successively.

Their other major need is rich soil. The big leaves and flowers quite naturally will need plenty of food. Avoid having a soil container which is too small. A good size container would be a wooden box about 12 inches square and 10 to 12 inches deep. Fill the box with a soil mixture, consisting of one part well-rotted cow manure, 3 parts soil and one handful of a commercial complete fertilizer. Next set the lily root 2 to 3 inches down in the mixture. Usually the tropical varieties will have been in the pots a few weeks before you buy them, and will already have several leaves. Be sure to plant these without disturbing the ball of earth surrounding them.

Set the box into a pool or quiet section of a stream so the crown of the root is 3 inches below the water surface, allowing 2½ to 3 feet square of water surface for each plant. The crown of the root is the point where the leaves and roots come forth. As the plant grows, lower the box an inch or so from time to time.

In the Winter, set the planting boxes containing the hardy water lilies on the pool floor, making sure the root crown is safely below the ice line. Many pools will be too shallow, so you will have to carry the boxes into a cool cellar for the Winter and keep the soil moist. Be sure to keep the boxes where the mice cannot get to them.

It is a good plan to protect the pool in winter by placing a log into the water to absorb ice expansion.

Aquatic Plants

No pool is complete without a water lily

Floating Plants —

These floating plants, by their foliage and blooms, provide a restful, natural backdrop for the more spectacular beauty of the lotus blossoms, water lilies and darting goldfish. They lend themselves well to pool arrangement, being attractive around the perimeter or in floating clusters among the blooms.

Duckweed — Tiny floating plants with leaves the size and shape of match heads. Dangling roots are excellent forage for fish, and they enjoy it.

Water Hyacinth—Inflated leaf petioles enable this plant to float and flourish with or without its roots in soil. Lavender blue blooms are attractive and are easily grown in aquariums or pools.

Water Poppy — A small plant that produces large yellow three-petaled poppies. Roots should be planted in soil. These plants are good in indoor tanks and aquariums and also outdoor pools.

Water Lettuce — Also known as Shell Flower. It has delightful rosettes of light blue-green hairy foliage that float. It is good for shade positions in the pool — but is killed by the frost.

OXYGENATING PLANTS

Oxygenating plants serve a triple purpose. Under the influence of light they give off oxygen, which is utilized by the fish. They provide splendid spawning material for the fish, and lend green freshness to pools and aquariums.

Cabomba — Roots easily, and its bright green, fanlike leaves grow rapidly. It is an excellent spawning plant, and one of the best of the oxygenators.

Myriophyllum — Fine hair-like leaves are ideal for receiving spawn of goldfish. This plant grows most beautifully in outdoor tanks or pools.

Anacharis — One of the finest submerged aquatics for fish culture and for the aquarium. It is a splendid spawn receiver, but spreads rapidly, so must be controlled in ponds or pools.

SHALLOW WATER PLANTS

These are marginal plants, for the most part, which sink their roots into the soil in shallow water. Most of them are on the large side — some bear blooms, some do not. The foliage of all of them is interesting and very decorative.

Giant Arrow-Head — A hardy plant from 1 to 3 feet tall. It produces big spikes of white flowers.

Common Cattail — A native American swamp plant, and one of the most nostalgic in practically any part of the country. It is easy to grow, very large, hardy and ornamental.

Parrot Feather — A favorite in pools, aquariums and in fountain bases. It has light green feathery leaves that grow in whorls, and can be made to droop over the edge of the basin.

Water Plantain — The water plantain is beautiful when planted around the shallow edges of a pool or pond. Bears tall branching spikes of white flowers, and the heart-shaped leaves are also very attractive.

Pickerel Rush — Is a free blooming native aquatic plant, and one of the very best for shallow water. Its flowers are blue, and cover a close-set spike. A healthy, hardy grower.

Sagittaria — A luxuriant growth for margins of ponds and streams, and also good in aquariums. The leaves are bright green and almost grass-like. Flowers are pure white.

Marsh Marigold — Especially adapted for wet ground around the edge of a pool. Bears clusters of bright yellow flowers which bloom in the early Spring.

Water Cress — A good plant for the edge of a running stream. It provides a welcome change of diet for both fish and humans. The water cress has dark green foliage and small white flowers.

Goldfish

Don't overfeed your goldfish

If you want to test your will power, sit beside a garden pool and try not to watch for the goldfish. You will find it most difficult, for goldfish have a fascination and a friendliness that few people can resist, whether the goldfish live in a small bowl, an aquarium or an outdoor pool.

Goldfish are the loved pets of more people throughout the world than any other living things. There are as many different sizes, shapes and colors of them as there are of cats, dogs, birds or any other pet and their habits are as diversified and interesting. There are shy ones, bold ones, fast ones and slow ones, exotically beautiful ones and goldfish so lovably ugly they make you laugh. They can be trained to come when you signal for them (by splashing) at mealtime.

They are inexpensive, no trouble to care for, and the business of keeping them is clean and tidy enough to suit the most fastidious housekeeper.

They are an asset to your water lily pool in some very practical ways. The web of life in the pool functions around an exchange between plant and animal life. The fish use oxygen from the water and return carbondioxide. The plants use carbondioxide and release oxygen. A pool cannot support a natural balance in any other way. Goldfish are good policemen too. Still water attracts mosquitoes. Fish eat both mosquitoes and eggs.

Remember these simple *Don'ts* and your fish will thrive and give you constant pleasure: *Don't* overstock your pool. Figure your pool water surface (pay no attention to floating greenery) in square inches, then put in 1 inch of goldfish (not counting the

Don't overstock your pool with fish

Shubunkin — A newer variety, with a colorful pattern as distinctive as fingerprints. Shubunkins are marked beautifully with patches of red, black, blue, yellow and brown on a pearl or pale blue background, and no two are alike. Many Shubunkins are nearly scaleless, many are entirely so.

Common Goldfish —This is the parent of all other goldfish varieties. It is not born with its beautiful color, and only half of each spawn attains perfect hue the first year. Life span in aquarium is months to several years, in pools 15 to 20 years. Sure death for mosquitoes.

Japanese Fantail — The Japanese Fantail is one of the most beautiful of fishes. This slow swimming Fantail will attract more attention than any other fish in your pool or aquarium.

Comet — The Comet's long tail and fins make him the fastest, most graceful of all goldfish. Beautiful color, coupled with his darting style of swimming, makes him a must addition to any pool.

tail) for every 20 square inches of water surface. Thus, a 5-inch fish would require 200 square inches — a space 10 by 20 inches. *Don't* overfeed. Sprinkle fish food upon the water according to directions on the label. Observe the fish, and thereafter give them only the amount of food they can eat in 5 minutes. Feed them once daily. When you leave home for a few days, let them miss the meals — and do not make them up. They may have an added treat now and then — small insects, earthworms.

In the warmer parts of the country the hardy varieties of goldfish will winter in an outdoor pool quite well and need to be fed lightly only once a week — if at all. If ice forms on the pool, make some openings to let in the air. This is best done with a tea-kettle full of hot water — the steam will melt the holes through the ice very neatly. The shock of breaking the ice might injure the fish.

In the colder areas it may be necessary to keep the fish over winter in an indoor aquarium in the home, or have them kept in one of the local commercial ones.

VARIETIES

Calico — The Calico is one of the most beautiful of the goldfish. It is similar in hue and markings to the Shubunkin, but has considerably more fin and tail development. It has the added interest of continuing to develop for months, even years, attaining peak beauty with maturity.

Frogs, Tadpoles and Snails — Frogs are always a sound investment that provide your pool with not only interest, but with some of Nature's music. Tadpoles are splendid pool scavengers, and contrary to popular thought, they do not eat fish eggs. Snails are also very useful for keeping the water clear of scum and come in several species.

89

Rock Gardens

One of the most eye-catching parts of the garden can be the rock garden

Rocks should not be placed in strict geometric patterns

Petunias bring summer beauty to a rock garden

When planting, tamp the soil firmly around the roots to remove air pockets

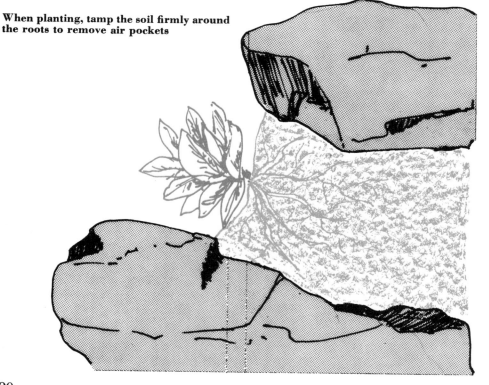

One of the most eye catching and charming parts of any garden can be the rock garden. It will provide a great deal of enjoyment for many home gardeners, not only in the designing and building of the rock garden, but in the day by day care which it will most surely need.

However, just because you have a garden does not mean that you should have or need a rock garden. Before being carried away by the idea you should ask yourself — "Will it fit into my garden without the overall effect being unnatural?" "Have I a suitable bank or slope I can use for making this type of garden?" "Where can I get the natural rock material?"

The maintenance of a rock garden, to keep it attractive during the entire growing season and to have a continuous supply of bloom from March until the heavy frosts of Fall requires much hard work and a lot of time. Just neglect your rock garden for one season and the weeds will take over.

A rock wall is softened by planting flowers along the top and the bottom

Unless you are an experienced home gardener, it is advisable to call in an expert landscape firm to do the job. Check over the firm's qualifications carefully before you give them a contract.

The ideal site for a rock garden is the side of a winding and sloping ravine. This will provide the perfect situation for almost any plant you would want to grow in the rock garden. Other successful locations could be a series of raised beds 1 to 4 feet high, with winding walks in between.

Very often the slope of land formed to hide the front of the foundation can be used to good effect. In this type of location there is a tendency, when the rocks are placed in position by the amateur, to have them in strict geometric patterns which do not look natural and can, in fact, be unsightly. Try to imitate nature and the results can be most pleasing.

In some parts of the country there are existing rock outcrops which can be the nucleus of the rock garden. Any additional work that is done in such cases must be in complete harmony with the existing landscape.

GRAVEL

BROKEN STONE

Pools and rock gardens make a happy combination

A gentle slope is an ideal location for a rock garden

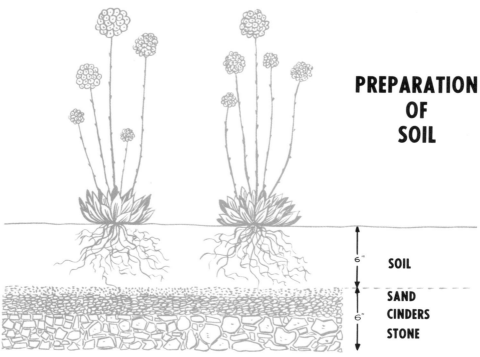

PREPARATION OF SOIL

SOIL

SAND
CINDERS
STONE

Many of the gardens in new subdivisions are completely level, and it is rather hard to give the rock garden a natural setting.

It is true you can mound up earth in a part of the garden, but no matter how well it is constructed, it would still look out of place. You can counteract this by making a planting of shrubs and evergreens which will not only provide a suitable background for the rock garden but will also serve as a partial screen.

Before building your own rock garden or hiring someone else to do it you would be well advised to look over the better rock gardens near where you live. Your local garden club, horticultural society or nurseryman should be able to tell you where these are located.

When you visit them, take note of how they blend into the landscape, and how the rocks will appear as if they had been there for many years. Also observe the amount of rock showing above the surface of the soil. In many cases only 1/3 of it is visible, while 2/3 is buried.

The kind of rocks to use depends on those available in the part of the country in which you live. Although weathered rocks of almost any kind can be used to make an attractive rock garden, there is no doubt that

Pockets in the rock garden should be constructed so that the plants seem to flow down over the rocks

You can plant most dwarf flowers in the pocket of a rock garden

Before building a rock garden check the better ones near where you live

A rock garden is made up of many tiny gardens

weathered limestone or irregular shapes and containing many small holes and pockets will make the most natural rock garden.

Home gardeners who want to do the job themselves, very often take a particular delight in collecting rocks from around the countryside. Whether you collect them personally or buy them from a landscape firm, make sure you do not have rocks all of the approximate shape and size. Even in the smaller rock gardens you will need big rocks that one person will have trouble in moving. The larger ones are necessary to use up some of the height of the bank. Without them it would be almost impossible to have a successful rock garden.

You will also need an equal number of medium sized rocks that are fairly easy to handle, and a good supply of small ones. These would be used mainly to prevent the soil from being eroded and washed out of the pockets.

In building a rock garden we are trying to imitate what we find in the woods. Here you never see a group of stones on end, or in a straight line, and it should be the same in our gardens.

The person starting out to build a rock garden must first of all learn to recognize

In order to grow many of the rarer rock plants you will need to duplicate the soil conditions in which they grow naturally

The best way to water a rock garden is to use a soaker hose to get into the pockets.

what is called the "face" of a rock. Believe it or not, each one has a face and this can be best described simply as the way the rock looks best when set in the soil.

Until you get the knack of it, you may have to move a rock several times until you notice which way it faces or looks best. If this does not come easily, perhaps you could visit a local rock garden expert and get him to give you a demonstration. Again, a visit to a recognized well-constructed rock garden would be worthwhile.

You could say a rock garden is made up of many tiny gardens, which consist of soil surrounded by rocks. The soil in each one will be suited to the needs of the particular plant you wish to grow there. This does not necessarily apply to many of the familiar low-growing perennials such as aubretia, alyssum, campanula, etc., which to all intents and purposes have the same soil requirements.

As you become more proficient in rock gardening you will want to tackle some of the rarer alpine plants such as the various saxifrages and others which come from many parts of the world. In order to have these grow successfully you will have to duplicate as nearly as possible the soil conditions in which they grow naturally.

Some of them may like a sandy, dry soil, others may prefer a soil which contains plenty of humus to keep it moist at all times.

Before starting to build the rock garden, all the existing top-soil should be removed and the sub-soil underneath graded to fit the desired contours of the finished rock garden.

For the beginner to rock gardening, here are some fool-proof perennial rock garden plants with the color of the flower and the time of flowering.

Carpet phlox and yellow alyssum are two of the easiest to grow rock plants

Rock Garden Plants

Name	Color	Flowering time
Alyssum (Cloth of Gold) (Saxatile Compactum)	Yellow	May
Arabis	Double flowered white Single flowers white Single pink	April to May
Alpine Aster (Alpinus)	Purplish-blue	May and June
Bluebells (Mertensia)	Deep blue	May
Candytuft (Iberis)	White	June
Campanula Carpatica	Porcelain blue	July to September
Campanula Garganica	Bright blue	July
Dianthus Caesius Cheddar	Bright pink	June
Dianthus Plumarius	White and pinks	June
Dwarf Michaelmas Daisies	Pink, blue, purple	September to October
Dwarf Iris	Red, light and dark blue, lilac, purple	June
Geum	Orange-red	June to July
Hepatica	Double pink	May
Heuchera (Coral Bells)	Coral red, scarlet	June to July
Lychnis (Campion) (Viscaria splendens)	Bright scarlet	July to September
Saxifraga	White	May to June
Sedum (Stonecrop)	Yellows, pinks, reds	June to September
Thyme	White, pink, crimson	June to July
Veronica	Bright blue	July
Viola	Apricot, blue, yellow, red	June to July

Dwarf iris make fine rock garden plants

Other flowers for the rock garden

The natural flowering time for most of the true rock plants and alpines is from early Spring until the middle of June. From then on you will have to use small annuals and the Spring flowering bulbs to keep a show of bloom coming along.

SMALL ANNUALS FOR THE ROCK GARDEN

Name	Color
Sweet alyssum	Pink, white, purple
Ageratum	Blue, white
Anchusa	Blue
Calliopsis (Dwarf annual)	Yellow, orange mahogany, brown, crimson
Cockscomb (Celosia Cristata)	Red, yellow, orange, crimson, rose and red
Cynoglossum (Chinese forget-me-nots)	Dwarf blue
Dianthus (Annual pinks)	White, pink, rose, scarlet
Lobelia	Blue
Dwarf marigolds	Orange, yellow, mahogany, red
Nasturtiums (Dwarf giant, double and single)	Rose, yellow, orange and scarlet
Nierembergia (Blue cup flower)	Lavender blue, violet blue
Phlox (Dwarf annual)	White, primrose, pink and reds
Zinnias — Little Cupid	Mixed colors
Zinnias — Tom Thumb	Mixed colors
Verbenas	Red, pinks, white

LITTLE SPRING FLOWERING BULBS FOR THE ROCK GARDEN

Name	Color
Winter aconite	Yellow
Snowdrops	White
Crocus	White, purple and yellow
Chiondoxa	Sky blue
Iris Reticulata	Deep violet, yellow
Grape hyacinth	Blue, white
Scilla	Blue, white, pink
Puschkinia	Gray-blue
Miniature daffodils	Yellow, white
Dwarf tulips —	
Greigi	Red, orange, dark pink, yellow and white
Kaufmanniana	Creamy white, marked with carmine
Fosteriana	Vermilion, hybrids.
Praestans	Scarlet

EVERGREENS FOR THE ROCK GARDEN

For the larger pockets in the rock garden, there are several varieties of permanently dwarf and upright evergreens that can be used to advantage:

   Dwarf Japanese yew
   Old Gold Pfitzer juniper
   Andorra juniper
   Hedgehog spruce
   Nest spruce
   Dwarf white spruce

BROAD LEAVED EVERGREENS

   Daphne or Garland Flower
   Euonymus Emerald Cushion